S · N · BEHRMAN

END OF SUMMER

A PLAY IN THREE ACTS

RANDOM HOUSE · NEW YORK

COPYRIGHT, 1936, BY S. N. BEHRMAN

CAUTION: Professionals and amateurs are hereby warned that "End of Summer," being fully protected under the Copyright Laws of the United States of America, the British Empire, including the Dominion of Canada, and all other countries of the Copyright Union, is subject to royalty. All rights, including professional, amateur, motion picture, recitation, lecturing, public reading, radio broadcasting, and the rights of translation into foreign languages are strictly reserved. Particular emphasis is laid on the question of readings, permission for which must be secured from the author's agent in writing. All inquiries should be addressed to the author's agent, Harold Freedman, 101 Park Avenue, New York City.

PRINTED IN THE UNITED STATES OF AMERICA

For

MAY AND HAROLD FREEDMAN

CHARACTERS

WILL DEXTER	SAM FROTHINGHAM
MRS. WYLER	DR. KENNETH RICE
PAULA FROTHINGHAM	DENNIS MCCARTHY
ROBERT	DR. DEXTER
LEONIE FROTHINGHAM	BORIS, COUNT MIRSKY

SCENE

The action of the play takes place in the living room of Bay Cottage, the Frothinghams' summer place in Northern Maine.

TIME

The present.

END OF SUMMER was produced by the Theatre Guild, Inc., at the Guild Theatre, New York, on Monday night, February 17, 1936, with the following cast:

(in the order of their appearance)

Will Dexter	Shepperd Strudwick
Mrs. Wyler	Mildred Natwick
Paula Frothingham	Doris Dudley
Robert	Kendall Clark
Leonie Frothingham	Ina Claire
Sam Frothingham	Minor Watson
Dr. Kenneth Rice	Osgood Perkins
Dennis McCarthy	Van Heflin
Dr. Dexter	Herbert Yost
Boris, Count Mirsky	Tom Powers

ACT ONE

ACT ONE

SCENE: *The verandah-living room of the Frothingham estate. Bay Cottage in Northern Maine. It is a charmingly furnished room with beautiful old distinguished pieces. A chintz couch and chairs give the room an air of informality. Beyond the door back you see a spacious, more formal room. Through the series of glass windows over the curving window seat on the right wall you see the early budding lilac and sumach. Woodbine and Virginia creeper are sprawling over the fence of native stone. Silver birch and maple are beginning to put out their leaves. The tops of red pine and cedar are visible over the rocks which fall away to the sea.*

Time: The present. A lovely afternoon in May.

At Rise: MRS. WYLER, *a very old lady and* WILL DEXTER, *an attractive, serious boy, are engaged in conversation.* MRS. WYLER *is knitting.*

WILL

When you were a young girl in Cleveland, did you see much of Mr. Rockefeller?

END OF SUMMER

MRS. WYLER

Not much. Of course my husband saw him every day at the office. But he never came to our house. We were young and worldly. He was strict and religious.

WILL

Did you suspect, in those days, how rich you were going to be?

MRS. WYLER

Mercy no! We debated a long time before we moved up to Cleveland from Oil City. My mother thought Oil City was no place to bring up a young girl. She finally persuaded my father to let us move up to Cleveland. But there was a lot of talk about the expense.

WILL

Was Oil City lively?

MRS. WYLER

[*Demurely.*]
It was pretty rough! I remember the celebration when they ran the first pipe-line through to Pittsburgh. That was a celebration!

WILL

The oil just poured, didn't it? Gushed out of the ground in great jets, and the people swarmed from everywhere to scoop it up.

END OF SUMMER

MRS. WYLER

I remember we had a gusher in our backyard. We put a fence around it to keep the cows from lapping up the oil.

WILL

Were you excited?

MRS. WYLER

Not by the oil.

WILL

I should think you would have been!

MRS. WYLER

[*Dryly.*]
We weren't. Oil was smelly. We wanted to get away from it. We discovered bath-salts.

WILL

You didn't know it was the true fountain of your—dynasty?

MRS. WYLER

We left it to the men—as I look back over my life the principal excitement came from houses—buying and building houses. The shack in Oil City to the mansion on Fifth Avenue. We had houses everywhere —houses in London, houses in Paris, Newport and this

—and yet, it seemed to me, we were always checking in and out of hotels.

WILL

It seems strange to think—

MRS. WYLER

What?

WILL

This golden stream—that you stumbled on so accidentally—it's flowing still—quenchless—and you on it—all you dynastic families—floating along in it—in luxurious barges!

MRS. WYLER

When I read these books about the early days of oil—these debunking books, you call them—they make me smile.

WILL

Do they? Why? I'd like to know that.

MRS. WYLER

They're so far from the truth.

WILL

Are they?

END OF SUMMER

MRS. WYLER

Of course they are!

WILL

Why?

MRS. WYLER

Because they're written from a foreign point of view—not *our* point of view. We did as well as anybody could have done according to our lights.

WILL

Yes, but what sort of lights were they?

MRS. WYLER

[*Tolerantly.*]
There you are!

WILL

How lucky you were!

MRS. WYLER

[*Teasing him.*]
Our young men didn't moon about. They made opportunities for themselves!

WILL

Or did the opportunities make them? All you had to do was pack your week-end bag and pioneer.

END OF SUMMER

MRS. WYLER

Is the world quite exhausted then?

WILL

Possibly not, but our pioneering might take a form you would find—unpalatable.

MRS. WYLER

Yes, yes.

[*Benevolently.*]

I suppose you're one of those young radicals our colleges are said to be full of nowadays. Tell me, what do you young radicals stand for?

WILL

I haven't decided exactly what I'm for, but I'm pretty certain what I'm against.

MRS. WYLER

[*Pumping him.*]

Most young people are bored by the past. You're full of curiosity. Why is that?

WILL

[*Not committing himself.*]

I'm interested.

END OF SUMMER

MRS. WYLER

At my age to be permitted to talk of one's youth is an indulgence. Ask me anything you like. At my age also one has no reason for restraint. I have had the bad judgment to survive most of my contemporaries.

WILL

I love talking to you, Mrs. Wyler. I think you're very wise.

MRS. WYLER

[*With a sigh.*]
Go on thinking so—I'll try not to disillusion you!
[*A moment's pause.*]
Are you staying on here at Bay Cottage?

WILL

Oh, no, I have to go back to Amherst to get my degree.

MRS. WYLER

And after that?

WILL

[*Humorously.*]
The dole!
[*The old lady laughs.*]

MRS. WYLER

My daughter tells me she's invited your father here.

END OF SUMMER

WILL

Yes.

MRS. WYLER

I shall be so glad to meet him. He's an inventor, isn't he?

WILL

He's a physicist. Specializes in—

MRS. WYLER

Don't tell me—in spite of my great wisdom I can't keep up with science. Whenever anybody makes a scientific explanation to me I find there are two things I don't know instead of just one.

WILL

[*Cheerfully.*]
Anyway, Dad's been fired.

MRS. WYLER

I am very sorry to hear that.

WILL

He's been working on a method for improving high-speed steel.

MRS. WYLER

Did he fail?

END OF SUMMER

WILL

He succeeded.

[Mrs. Wyler *is surprised.*]

They decided that his discovery, if perfected and marketed, might increase the technological unemployment. They have decided therefore to call a halt on scientific discovery—especially in those branches where it might have practical results. That is one of the differences, Mrs. Wyler, between my day—and yours—in your day, you put a premium on invention—we declare a moratorium on it.

[*The old lady gives him a shrewd look.*]

MRS. WYLER

Yes, yes. I am perfectly sure that you're in for a hard time, Will.

WILL

[*Lightly, shrugging his shoulders.*]

As I have been elected by my class as the one most likely to succeed, I am not worrying, Mrs. Wyler. All I have to do is bide my time.

MRS. WYLER

[*Amused.*]

I am perfectly certain you'll come out! Paula tells me you and your friend, Dennis McCarthy, want to start some kind of magazine.

END OF SUMMER

WILL

Yes. A national magazine for undergraduate America. You see, Mrs. Wyler, before the rift in our so-called system, college men were supposed to live exclusively in a world of ukuleles, football slogans, and petting-parties—*College Humor* sort of thing. But it was never entirely true. Now it is less true than ever. This magazine—if we can get it going—would be a forum for intercollegiate thought. It would be the organ of critical youth as opposed—to the other.

MRS. WYLER

What other?

WILL

The R.O.T.C., the Vigilantes and the Fascists—the Youth Movement of guns and sabres—

MRS. WYLER

I see. Well, I wish you luck, Will.

WILL

Thank you.

[PAULA FROTHINGHAM *comes in, a lovely young girl in gay summer slacks.*]

PAULA

[*To* WILL.]
Aren't you swimming? Hello, Granny.

WILL
Your grandmother and I have been discussing life.

PAULA
With a capital L, I suppose?

WILL
Enormous! I've been getting data on the pioneer age. Your grandmother thinks the reason we're in the condition we're in is because we're lazy.

MRS. WYLER
[*Mildly.*]
Lazy? Did I say that?

WILL
In a way.

MRS. WYLER
If I said it, it must be so. Everybody over seventy is infallible!

PAULA
[*Nestling to her.*]
Darling!

MRS. WYLER
Survival is quite a knack. You children don't realize it.

WILL
Oh, don't we though! It's getting harder every day.

END OF SUMMER

MRS. WYLER

Nonsense! At your age you can't help it.

WILL

In your stately opulence that's what you think, Mrs. Wyler. You just don't know!

MRS. WYLER

Nonsense! Do you think your generation has a monopoly on hard times?

WILL

Now please don't tell me we've had depressions before?

MRS. WYLER

[*Rising to go.*]
Paula, your young man is impertinent. Don't have anything to do with him.
[*She goes out.*]

PAULA

What a conquest you've made of Granny! Way and ahead of all my beaus!

WILL

That undistinguished mob! Who couldn't?

PAULA

As long as you admit there is a mob . . .

WILL

Why wouldn't there be? Everybody loves you for your money!

PAULA

[*Confidently.*]

I know it! And of all the fortune-hunters I've had dangling after me you're easily the most . . .

WILL

Blatant!

PAULA

That's it! Blatant! Like my new slacks?

WILL

Love 'em.

PAULA

Love me?

WILL

Loathe you.

PAULA

Good! Kiss?

[*They kiss quickly.*]

WILL

Funny thing about your grandmother . . .

PAULA

Now I won't have you criticising Granny . . .

WILL

I'm crazy about her. You feel she's been through everything and that she understands everything. Not this though. Not the essential difference between her times and ours.

PAULA

Oh, dear! Is it the end of the world then?

WILL

The end of this world.

PAULA

[*Goes to window seat right, with a sigh.*]
Such a pretty world.
   [*She points through windows at the garden and sea beyond.*]
Look at it! Too bad it has to go! Meantime before it quite dissolves let's go for a swim.
   [*She starts for door.*]

WILL

[*Abstracted.*]
All right. . . .
   [*Following her to window seat.*]

END OF SUMMER

PAULA
[*She turns back.*]
What's on your mind?

WILL
Wanted to speak to you about something. . . .

PAULA
What?

WILL
[*Embarrassed slightly.*]
Er—your mother. . . .

PAULA
What's Mother gone and done now? Out with it. Or is it you? My boy-friends are always in love with Mother. I've had to contend with that all my life. So if it's that you needn't even mention it . . . come on.

WILL
No, but really, Paula. . . .

PAULA
Well then, out with it! What is it!

WILL
This.
[*He gives her note.*]

END OF SUMMER

Found it on my breakfast tray this morning in a sealed envelope marked "Confidential."

PAULA

[*Reading note aloud, rather bewildered.*]
"To give my little girl a good time with. Leonie Frothingham."

WILL

And this!
[*He hands her check.* PAULA *takes it and looks at it.*]

PAULA

A hundred dollars. Does Mother think her little girl can have a good time with *that*? She doesn't know her little girl!

WILL

But what'll I do with it? How'll I get it back to her?

PAULA

Over my dead body you'll get it back to her! You'll spend it on Mother's little girl. Now come on swimming!

WILL

Does your mother put one of these on every breakfast tray?

END OF SUMMER

PAULA

Argue it out with her?

WILL

I can't. It would seem ungracious. You must give it back to her for me.

PAULA

Catch me! Don't take it too seriously. She slips all the kids something every once in a while. She knows my friends are all stony. You overestimate the importance of money, Will—it's a convenience, that's all. You've got a complex on it.

WILL

I have! I've got to have. It's all right to be dainty about money when you've lots of it as you have. . . .

PAULA

Rotten with it is the expression, I believe. . . .

WILL

I repudiate that expression. It is genteel and moralistic. You can't be rotten with money—you can only be *alive* with it.

PAULA

You and the rest of our crowd make me feel it's bad

taste to be rich. But what can I do? I didn't ask for it!

WILL

I know. But look here . . . I've got a brother out of college two years who's worked six weeks in that time and is broke and here I am in an atmosphere with hundred-dollar bills floating around!

PAULA

[*With check.*]
Send him that!

WILL

Misapplication of funds!

PAULA

[*Warmly.*]
Mother would be only too . . .

WILL

I know she would—but that isn't the point. . . . You know, Paula—

PAULA

What?

WILL

Sometimes I think if we weren't in love with each other we should be irreconcilable enemies—

END OF SUMMER

PAULA

Nothing but sex, eh?

WILL

That's all.

PAULA

In that case—
[*They kiss.*]

WILL

That's forgiving. But seriously, Paula—

PAULA

Seriously what?

WILL

I can't help feeling I'm here on false pretences. What am I doing with a millionaire family—with you? If your mother knew what I think, and what I've let you in for in college—she wouldn't touch me with a ten-foot pole. And you too—I'm troubled about the superficiality of your new opinions. Isn't your radicalism—acquired coloring?

PAULA

I hope not. But—so is all education.

WILL

I know but—!

END OF SUMMER

PAULA

What are you bleating about? Didn't I join you on that expedition to Kentucky to be treated by that sovereign state as an offensive foreigner? My back aches yet when I remember that terrible bus ride. Didn't I get my name in the papers picketing? Didn't I give up my holiday to go with you to the Chicago Peace Congress? Didn't I?

WILL

[*Doubtfully.*]
Yes, you did.

PAULA

But you're not convinced. Will darling, don't you realize that since knowing you and your friends, since I've, as you say, acquired your point of view about things, my life has had an excitement and a sense of reality it's never had before. I've simply come alive—that's all! Before then I was bored—terribly bored without knowing why. I wanted something more—fundamental—without knowing what. You've made me see. I'm terribly grateful to you, Will darling. I always shall be.

WILL

You are a dear, Paula, and I adore you—but—

PAULA

Still unconvinced?

WILL

This money of yours. What'll it do to us?

PAULA

I'll turn it over to you. Then you can give me an allowance—and save your pride.

WILL

I warn you, Paula—

PAULA

What?

WILL

If you turn it over to me, I'll use it in every way I can to make it impossible for anyone to have so much again.

PAULA

That's all right with me, Will.

WILL

Sometimes you make me feel I'm taking candy from babies.

PAULA

The candy is no good for the baby, anyway. Besides, let's cross that bridge when we come to it.

[ROBERT, *the butler, enters.*]

END OF SUMMER

ROBERT

I beg your pardon, Miss Frothingham.

PAULA

Yes, Robert?

ROBERT

Telephone for you.

PAULA

Thank you, Robert.
[*She crosses to table back of sofa for telephone.*]
[*At phone.*]
Yes—this is Paula—Dad!—Darling!—Where are you? . . . but how wonderful . . . I thought you were in New York . . . well, come right over this minute. . . . Will you stay the night? . . . Oh, too bad! . . . I'll wait right here for you. Hurry, darling! Bye!
[*She hangs up.*]
Imagine, dad! He's motoring up to Selena Bryant's at Murray Bay—I'm dying to have you meet him. He's the lamb of the world.

WILL

Not staying long, is he?

PAULA

No. He wants to see Mother he says. I wonder . . . oh, dear!

END OF SUMMER

WILL

What?

PAULA

I was so excited I forgot to tell him. . . .

WILL

What?

PAULA

That a new friend of Mother's is coming.

WILL

The Russian?

PAULA

The Russian's here. He dates from last winter. You're behind the times, Will.

WILL

Who's the new friend?

PAULA

I'm not sure about it all yet. Maybe Mother isn't either. But I've had some experience in watching them come and go and my instinct tells me Dr. Rice is elected.

WILL

Who is Dr. Rice?

PAULA

Psychoanalyst from New York.

END OF SUMMER

[*Burlesquing slightly.*]
The last word, my dear—
[*At this point the object of* PAULA'S *maternal impulse comes in, running a little and breathless, like a young girl.* LEONIE FROTHINGHAM, *as she has a daughter of nearly twenty, must be herself forty, but, at this moment, she might be sixteen. She is slim, girlish, in a young and quivering ecstasy of living and anticipation. For* LEONIE, *her daughter is an agreeable phenomenon whom she does not specially relate to herself biologically—a lovely apparition who hovers intermittently, in the wild garden of her life. There is something, for all her gaiety, heartbreaking about* LEONIE, *something childish and child-like—an acceptance of people instantly and uncritically at the best of their own valuation. She is impulsive and warm-hearted and generous to a fault. Her own fragile and exquisite loveliness she offers to the world half shyly, tentatively, bearing it like a cup containing a precious liquid of which not a drop must be spilled. A spirituelle amoureuse she is repelled by the gross or the voluptuary; this is not hypocrisy—it is, in* LEONIE, *a more serious defect than that. In the world in which she moves hypocrisy is merely a social lubricant but this myopia—alas for* LEONIE!—*springs from a*

congenital and temperamental inability to face anything but the pleasantest and the most immediately appealing and the most flattering aspects of things—in life and in her own nature. At this moment, though, she is the loveliest fabrication of Nature, happy in the summer sun and loving all the world.]

LEONIE

My darlings, did you ever know such a day?

WILL

[*He is a shy boy with her.*]
It's nice!

LEONIE

Nice! It's . . .
[*Her gesture conveys her utter inadequacy to express the beauties of the day.*]
It's—radiant! It knows it's radiant! The world is pleased with herself today. Is the world a woman? Today she is—a lovely young girl in blue and white.

WILL

In green and white.

LEONIE

[*Agreeing—warmly.*]

END OF SUMMER

In green and white!—It depends where you look, doesn't it? I'm just off to the station to meet Dr. Rice. Will, you'll be fascinated by him.

PAULA
[*Cutting in—crisply.*]
Sam telephoned.

LEONIE
Sam!

PAULA
Your husband. My father. Think back, Leonie.

LEONIE
Darling! Where is he?

PAULA
He's on his way here. He telephoned from Miller's Point.

LEONIE
Is he staying?

PAULA
No.

LEONIE
Why not?

END OF SUMMER

PAULA

He's going on to Selena Bryant's.

LEONIE

What is this deep friendship between Sam and Selena Bryant?

PAULA

Now Leonie, don't be prudish!

LEONIE

[*Appealing for protection to* WILL.]
She's always teasing me. She's always teasing everybody about everything. Developed quite a vein. I must warn you, Paula—sarcasm isn't feminine. In their heart of hearts men don't like it. Do you like it, Will? Do you really like it?

WILL

I hate it!

LEONIE

[*In triumph to* PAULA.]
There you see! He hates it!

PAULA

[*Tersely.*]
He doesn't always hate it!

LEONIE
[*Her most winning smile on* WILL.]
Does she bully you, Will? Don't let her bully you. The sad thing is, Paula, you're so charming. Why aren't you content to be charming? Are you as serious as Paula, Will? I hope not.

WILL
Much more.

LEONIE
I'm sorry to hear that. Still, for a man, it's all right, I suppose. But why are the girls nowadays so determined not to be feminine? Why? It's coming back you know—I'm sure of it—femininity is due for a revival.

PAULA
So are Herbert Hoover and painting on china.

LEONIE
Well I read that even in Russia . . . the women . . .
[*She turns again to* WILL *whom she feels sympathetic.*]
It isn't as if women had done such marvels with their —masculinity! Have they? Are things better because women vote? Not that I can see. They're worse. As far as I can see the women simply reinforce the men in their—mistakes.

END OF SUMMER

WILL

[*To* PAULA.]
She has you there!

LEONIE

[*With this encouragement warming to her theme.*]
When I was a girl the calamities of the world were on a much smaller scale. It's because the women, who, after all, are half of the human race, stayed at home and didn't bother. Now they do bother—and look at us!

PAULA

Well, that's as Victorian as anything I ever—

LEONIE

I'd love to have been a Victorian. They were much happier than we are, weren't they? Of course they were.

PAULA

[*Defending herself to* WILL.]
It's only Mother that brings out the crusader in me—
[*To* LEONIE.]
When you're not around I'm not like that at all. Am I, Will?

[*But* WILL *is given no chance to answer because* LEONIE *is holding a sprig of lilac to his nostrils.*]

LEONIE
Smell.

[WILL *smells.*]
Isn't it delicious?

WILL
It's lovely.

LEONIE
Here . . . .

[*She breaks off a sprig and pins it into his lapel. While she is doing it she broaches a delicate subject quite casually to* PAULA.]

Oh, by the way, Paula . . .

PAULA
Yes, Mother?

LEONIE
Did you mention to Sam that—that Boris—

PAULA
I didn't, no. It slipped my mind.

LEONIE
It doesn't matter in the least.

PAULA
Father isn't staying anyway . . .

END OF SUMMER

LEONIE

Well, why shouldn't he? You must make him. I want him to meet Dr. Rice. He's really a most extraordinary man.

PAULA

Where'd you *find him?*

LEONIE

I met him at a party at Sissy Drake's. He *saved* Sissy.

PAULA

From what?

LEONIE

From that awful eye-condition.

PAULA

Is he an oculist too?

LEONIE

[*To* WILL.]

She went to every oculist in the world—she went to Baltimore and she went to Vienna. Nobody could do a thing for her—her eyes kept blinking—twitching really in the most unaccountable way. It was an ordeal to talk to her—and of course she must have undergone agonies of embarrassment. But Dr. Rice psychoanalyzed her and completely cured her. How do you suppose? Well, he found that the seat of the trouble lay in her unconscious. It was too simple. She blinked in that awful way because actually she couldn't bear to look at her husband. So she divorced Drake and since she's married to Bill Wilmerding she's as normal as you or me. Now I'll take you into a little secret. I'm having Dr. Rice up to see Boris. Of course Boris mustn't know it's for him.

PAULA

What's the matter with Boris?

LEONIE

I'm not sure. I think he's working too hard.

WILL

What's he working at?

LEONIE

Don't you know? Didn't you tell him, Paula? His father's memoirs. He's the son, you know, of the great Count Mirsky!

WILL

I know.

LEONIE

I must show you the photographs of his father— wonderful old man with a great white beard like a snow-storm—looks like Moses—a Russian Moses—and Boris is sitting on his knees—couldn't be over ten years old and wearing a fur cap and boots—boots!—and they drank tea out of tall glasses with raspberry jelly in—people came from all over the world, you know, to see his father . . . !

WILL

Isn't it strange that Count Mirsky's son should find himself in this strange house on this odd headland of Maine—Maine of all places!—writing his father's life? It's fantastic!

PAULA

[*With some malice.*]
Is Dr. Rice going to help you acclimate him?

LEONIE

I hope so. You and Paula will have to entertain him—you young intellectuals. Isn't it a pity I have no mind?
[*She rises and crosses to table right to arrange lily-of-the-valley sprigs in a vase.*]

PAULA

[*To* WILL.]
She knows it's her greatest asset. Besides she's a fake.

WILL

[*Gallantly.*]
I'm sure she is.

LEONIE

Thank you, my dears. It's gallant of you.
[*She crosses to* PAULA—*embraces her from behind.*]
But I'm not deceived. I know what Paula thinks of me—she looks down on me because I won't get interested in sociology. There never were any such things about when I was a girl. The trouble is one generation never has any perspective about another generation.

WILL

That's what your mother was saying to me just a little while ago.

LEONIE

Was she?
[*She sits left of* WILL.]
I'm sure though Mother and I are much closer—that is, we understand each other better than Paula and I. Don't you think so, Paula?

PAULA

[*Considering it.*]
Yes. I do think so.

END OF SUMMER

LEONIE

I knew you'd agree. Something's happened between my generation and Paula's. New concepts. I don't know what they are exactly but I'm very proud that Paula's got them.

PAULA

[*Laughing helplessly.*]
Oh, Mother! You reduce everything to absurdity!

LEONIE

[*Innocently.*]
Do I? I don't mean to. At any rate it's a heavenly day and I adore you and I don't care about anything so long as you're happy. I want you to be happy.

PAULA

[*Helplessly.*]
Oh dear!

LEONIE

What's the matter?

PAULA

You're saying that!

LEONIE

Is that wrong? Will—did I say something wrong?

END OF SUMMER

PAULA

You want me to be happy. It's like saying you want me to be eight feet tall and to sing like Lily Pons.

LEONIE

Is it like that? Why? Will . . .

WILL

[*Gravely feeling he must stand up for* PAULA, *but hating to.*]
Paula means . . .
[*Pause.*]

LEONIE

Yes . . . ?

WILL

[*Miserable.*]
She means—suppose there isn't any happiness to be had? Suppose the supply's run out?

LEONIE

But, Will, really . . . ! On a day like this! Why don't you go swimming?
[*Rises.*]
Nothing like sea-water for—morbidity! Run out indeed! And today of all days! Really!
[*Gets gloves.*]

I'm disappointed in you, Will. I counted on you especially . . .

WILL

[*Abjectly.*]
I was only fooling!

LEONIE

Of course he was.
[*Sits on arm of sofa beside* WILL.]
Will, I rely on you. Don't let Paula brood. Can't she drop the sociology in the summer? I think in the fall you're much better—braced—for things like that. Keep her happy, Will.

WILL

I'll do my best now that—thanks to you—I have the means.

LEONIE

Oh. . . .
[*Remembering.*]
Oh, you didn't mind, did you? I hope you didn't mind.

WILL

[*Embarrassed.*]
Very generous of you.

LEONIE

Generous! Please don't say that. After all—we who are in the embarrassing position nowadays of being rich must do something with our money, mustn't we? That's why I'm helping Boris to write this book. *Noblesse oblige.* Don't you think so, Will? Boris tells me that the Russians—the *present* Russians—

WILL

You mean the Bolsheviks?

LEONIE

Yes, I suppose I do. He says they don't like his father at all any more and won't read his works because in his novels he occasionally went on the assumption that rich people had souls and spirits too. You don't think like that too, do you, Will—that because I'm rich I'm just not worth bothering about at all— No, you couldn't!

[*The appeal is tremulous.* WILL *succumbs entirely.*]

WILL

[*Bluntly.*]
Mrs. Frothingham, I love you!

LEONIE

[*Rises from arm of sofa and sits in sofa beside* WILL. *To* PAULA.]

Isn't he sweet?

[*To* WILL.]

And I love you, Will. Please call me Leonie. Do you know how Mother happened to name me Leonie? I was born in Paris, you know, and I was to be called Ruhama after my father's sister. But Mother said no. No child of mine, she said, shall be called Ruhama. She shall have a French name. And where do you think she got Leonie?

WILL

From the French version of one of those Gideon Bibles.

LEONIE

[*As breathless as if it happened yesterday.*]

Not at all. From a novel the nurse was reading. She asked the nurse what she was reading and the nurse gave her the paper book and Mother opened it and found Leonie!

WILL

What was the book?

LEONIE

Everyone wants to know that . . . But I don't know. Mother didn't know. She kept the book to give to me when I grew up. But one day she met M. Jusserand on

END OF SUMMER

a train—he was the French Ambassador to Washington, you know—and he picked up the book in Mother's compartment and he read a page of it and threw it out of the window because it was trash! You see what I've had to live down.

WILL

Heroic!

LEONIE

I hope you stay all summer, Will. I won't hear of your going anywhere else.

WILL

Don't worry. I have nowhere else to go!

LEONIE

Tell me—that magazine you and Dennis want to start—will it be gay?

WILL

Not exactly.

LEONIE

Oh, dear! I know. Columns and columns of reading matter and no pictures. Tell me—your father is coming to dine, isn't he? I am so looking forward to meeting him. I love scientific men. They're usually

so nice and understanding. Now, I've really got to go.
[*Rises and starts out.*]

PAULA

Dennis will be on that train.

LEONIE

Oh, good! I like Dennis. He makes me laugh and I like people around who make me laugh, but I do wish he'd dress better. Why can't radicals be chic? I saw a picture of Karl Marx the other day and he looks like one of those advertisements before you take something. I'll look after Dennis, Will—save you going to the station—

[*To* PAULA.]

And Paula, tell Sam—

PAULA

Yes?

LEONIE

[*Forgetting the message to* SAM.]

You know, I asked Dr. Rice if he would treat me professionally and he said I was uninteresting to him because I was quite normal. Isn't that discouraging? Really, I must cultivate something. Good-bye, darlings.

[*She runs out.*]

WILL

But what was the message to Sam?
[*He sits.*]

PAULA

[*Helplessly.*]
I'll never know. Neither will she.
[WILL *laughs.*]
What can you do with her? She makes me feel like an opinionated old woman. And I worry about her.

WILL

Do you?

PAULA

Yes. She arouses my maternal impulse.

WILL

[*Who feels he can be casual about* LEONIE *now that she is gone.*]
She relies rather too much on charm!

PAULA

[*Turning on him bitterly.*]
Oh, she does, does she!
[*Goes over to sofa and sits right of* WILL.]
You renegade. You ruin all my discipline with Mother. You're like a blushing schoolboy in front of her . . .

WILL

[*Protesting sheepishly.*]
Now, Paula, don't exaggerate!

PAULA

You are! I thought in another minute you were going to ask her to the frat dance. And where was all that wonderful indignation about her leaving you the check? Where was the insult to your pride? Where was your starving brother in Seattle? Where? Where?

WILL

I don't know but somehow you can't face your mother with things like that. It seems cruel to face her with realities. She seems outside of all that.

PAULA

[*Conceding that.*]
Well, you're going to be no help to me in handling Mother, I can see that!

WILL

[*Changing subject—a bit sensitive about having yielded so flagrantly to* LEONIE.]
This Russian—

PAULA

What about him?

END OF SUMMER

WILL
[*Gauche.*]
Platonic, do you suppose?

PAULA
Don't be naïve!
[*Enter* SAM FROTHINGHAM, PAULA's *father, a very pleasant-faced, attractive man between forty-five and fifty.*]

SAM
Oh, hello.
[WILL *rises.*]

PAULA
[*Flying to him.*]
Darling!—

SAM
[*They meet center and embrace.*]
Hello, Paula. Delighted to see you.

PAULA
This is Will Dexter.

SAM
[*Shaking hands with* WILL.]
How do you do?

WILL
I'm delighted to meet you.

PAULA
[*To* WILL.]
Wait for me at the beach, will you, Will?

WILL
No, I'll run down to the station and ride back with the others.

PAULA
Okay.
[SAM *nods to him.* WILL *goes out.*]

SAM
[*Crosses to front of sofa.*]
Nice boy.
[*Follows her.*]

PAULA
Like him?

SAM
Do you?

PAULA
I think so.

SAM
Special?

PAULA

Sort of.

SAM

Very special?

PAULA

[*Sits right end of sofa.*]
Well—not sure.

SAM

Wait till you are. You've lots of time.

PAULA

Oh, he's not exactly impulsive.

SAM

Then he's just a fool.

PAULA

How are you, darling?

SAM

Uneasy.

PAULA

With me!

SAM

Especially.

PAULA

Darling, why?

SAM

I'll tell you. That's why I've come.

PAULA

Everything all right?

SAM

Oh, fine.

PAULA

[*Mystified.*]
Then . . . ?

SAM

[*Switching off.*]
How's Leonie?

PAULA

Fine. Delighted you were coming.

SAM

Was she?

PAULA

She really was. She's off to Ellsworth to meet a doctor.

SAM

Doctor?

END OF SUMMER

PAULA

Psychoanalyst she's having up to massage her Russian's complexes.

SAM

[*Laughing.*]
Oh—
[*With a sigh.*]
What's going to happen to Leonie?

PAULA

Why? She's on the crest!

SAM

She needs that elevation. Otherwise she sinks.

PAULA

Well—you know Mother . . .

SAM

Yes.
[*A moment's pause.*]
Paula?

PAULA

Yes, dad.

SAM

The fact is—it's ridiculous I should feel so nervous about telling you—but the fact is . . .

PAULA

What?

SAM

I've fallen in love. I want to get married. There! Well, thank God that's out!

[*He wipes his forehead, quite an ordeal.*]

Romance at my age. It's absurd, isn't it?

PAULA

Selena Bryant?

SAM

Yes.

PAULA

She has a grown son.

SAM

[*Smiling at her.*]

So have I—a grown daughter.

PAULA

You'll have to divorce Mother.

SAM

Yes.

PAULA

Poor Leonie!

SAM

Well, after all—Leonie—you know how we've lived for years.

PAULA

Has Leonie hurt you?

SAM

Not for a long time. If this with Selena hadn't happened we'd have gone on forever, I suppose. But it has.

PAULA

You know, I have a feeling that, in spite of everything, this is going to be a shock to Leonie.

SAM

Paula?

PAULA

Yes.

SAM

Do you feel I'm deserting you?
[*She turns her head away. She is very moved.*]

PAULA

No—you know how fond I am of you—I want you to be . . .

SAM

[*Deeply affected.*]
Paula . . . !

END OF SUMMER

PAULA
Happy.
[*A silence. She is on the verge of tears.*]

SAM
I must make you see my side, Paula.

PAULA
[*Vehemently.*]
I do!

SAM
It isn't only that—you're so young—but somehow—we decided very soon after you were born, Leonie and I, that our marriage could only continue on this sort of basis. For your sake we've kept it up. I thought I was content to be an—appendage—to Leonie's entourage. But I'm not—do you know what Selena—being with Selena and planning with Selena for ourselves has made me see—that I've never had a home. Does that sound mawkish?

PAULA
I thought you loved Bay Cottage.

SAM
Of our various menages this is my favorite—it's the simplest. And I've had fun here with you—watching

you grow up. But very soon after I married Leonie I found this out—that when you marry a very rich woman it's always *her* house you live in.

[*A moment's pause.*]

PAULA

I'm awfully happy for you, Sam, really I am. You deserve everything but I can't help it I . . .

SAM

I know.
[*A pause.*]
Paula . . .

PAULA

Yes, dad?

SAM

You and I get on so well together—always have—Selena adores you and really—when you get to know her . . .

PAULA

I like Selena enormously. She's a dear. Couldn't be nicer.

SAM

I'm sure you and she would get on wonderfully together. Of course, Leonie will marry again. She's bound to. Why don't you come to live with us? When you want to . . .

END OF SUMMER

PAULA
Want to!

SAM
All the time then. Leonie has such a busy life.

PAULA
It's awfully sweet of you.

SAM
Sweet of me! Paula!

PAULA
Where are you going to live?

SAM
New York. Selena has her job to do.

PAULA
She's terribly clever, isn't she?

SAM
She's good at her job.

PAULA
It must be wonderful to be independent. I hope I shall be. I hope I can make myself.

END OF SUMMER

SAM

No reason you can't.

PAULA

It seems to take so much—

SAM

What sort of independence?

PAULA

Leonie's independent, but that independence doesn't mean anything somehow. She's always been able to do what she likes.

SAM

So will you be.

PAULA

That doesn't count somehow. It's independence in a vacuum. No, it doesn't count.

SAM

Maybe it isn't independence you want then?

PAULA

Yes, it is. I want to be able to stand on my own feet. I want to be—justified.

END OF SUMMER

SAM

[*Understandingly.*]
Ah! That's something else.
[*A little amused.*]
That's harder!

PAULA

I mean it, really I do—
[*Pause.*]
It's curious—how—adrift—this makes me feel. As if something vital, something fundamental had smashed. I wonder how Mother'll take it. I think—unconsciously—she depends on you much more than she realizes. You were a stabilizing force, Sam, in spite of everything and now . . .

SAM

[*Seriously.*]
You are the stabilizing force, if you ask me, Paula . . .

PAULA

I don't know.

SAM

What's worrying you, Paula? Is it this Russian?

PAULA

Oh, I think he's harmless really.

SAM

What then?

PAULA

That one of these days—

SAM

What?

PAULA

That one of these days—now that you're going—somebody will come along—who won't be harmless.—You know, I really love Leonie.

[LEONIE *comes running in just ahead of* DR. KENNETH RICE, DENNIS *and* WILL. LEONIE *is in the gayest spirits.* DR. RICE *is handsome, dark, magnetic, quiet, masterful. He is conscious of authority and gives one the sense of a strange, genius-like intuition.* DENNIS *is a flamboyant Irishman, a little older than* WILL, *gawky, black-haired, slovenly, infinitely brash.* SAM *and* PAULA *rise.* LEONIE *comes down to center with* KENNETH *at her left.* WILL *remains back of sofa.* DENNIS *follows down to right center.*]

LEONIE

Oh, Sam, how perfectly . . . This is Dr. Rice—my husband Sam Frothingham—and my daughter Paula! Sam, Dennis McCarthy.

END OF SUMMER

DENNIS
How do you do?
[*No one pays any attention to him.* DR. RICE *shakes hands with* SAM *and* PAULA. LEONIE *keeps bubbling, her little laugh tinkling through her chatter.*]

LEONIE
It's courageous of me, don't you think, Dr. Rice, to display such a daughter? Does she look like me? I'll be very pleased if you tell me that she does. Sit down, sit down, everybody.

DENNIS
[*Holding up his pipe.*]
You don't mind if I—?

LEONIE
No, no, not at all—
[*She sits center chair,* PAULA *sits on right end sofa,* DENNIS *sinks into chair, right, by table.*]
Sam! How well you're looking! Are you staying at Selena's? How is Selena?

SAM
She's very well.

LEONIE
Dr. Rice knows Selena.

KENNETH
Yes, indeed!

LEONIE
I envy Selena, you know, above all women. So brilliant, so attractive and so self-sufficient. That is what I envy in her most of all. I have no resources—I depend so much on other people.
[*Turns to* Rice.]
Do you think, Dr. Rice, you could make me self-sufficient?

KENNETH
I think I could.

LEONIE
How perfectly marvelous!

KENNETH
But I shouldn't dream of doing it!

LEONIE
But if I beg you to?

KENNETH
Not even if you beg me to.

LEONIE
But why?

KENNETH
It would deprive your friends of their most delightful avocation.

LEONIE
Now that's very grateful. You see, Sam, there are men who still pay me compliments.

SAM
I can't believe it!

LEONIE
You must keep it up, Dr. Rice, please. So good for my morale.
[*To* PAULA.]
Oh, my dear, we've been having the most wonderful argument—
[*To* DENNIS.]
Haven't we?

DENNIS
Yes.

LEONIE
All the way in from Ellsworth—
[*To* RICE.]
Really, Doctor, it's given me new courage . . .

PAULA

New courage for what?

LEONIE

I've always been afraid to say it for fear of being old-fashioned—but Dr. Rice isn't afraid.

KENNETH

[*Explaining to* SAM.]
It takes great courage, Mr. Frothingham, to disagree with the younger generation.

SAM

It does indeed.

PAULA

Well, what was it about?

LEONIE

Yes—what *was* it about, Dennis?

DENNIS

Statistics and theology. Some metaphysics thrown in.

SAM

Good heavens!
[*Sits.*]

END OF SUMMER

DENNIS

Statistics as a symbol.

WILL

Dr. Rice still believes in the individual career.

KENNETH

I hang my head in shame!

DENNIS

He doesn't know that as a high officer of the National Student Federation, I have at my fingers' ends the statistics which rule our future, the statistics which constitute our horizon. Not your future, Paula, because you are living parasitically on the stored pioneerism of your ancestors.

PAULA

Forgive me, Reverend Father!

DENNIS

I represent, Doctor, the Unattached Youth of America—

KENNETH

Well, that's a career in itself!
[*They laugh.*]

DENNIS

[*Imperturbable.*]

When we presently commit the folly of graduating from a benevolent institution at Amherst, Massachusetts, there will be in this Republic two million like us. Two million helots.

[*Leaning over* LEONIE.]

But Dr. Rice pooh-poohs statistics.

LEONIE

[*Arranging his tie.*]

Does he Dennis?

DENNIS

He says the individual can surmount statistics, violate the graphs. Superman!

WILL

Evidently Dr. Rice got in just under the wire.

KENNETH

I'd never submit to statistics, Mr. Dexter—I'd submit to many things but not to statistics.

LEONIE

Such dull things to submit to—

END OF SUMMER

DENNIS

You must be an atheist, Dr. Rice.

KENNETH

Because I don't believe in statistics?—the new God?

LEONIE

Well, *I'm* a Protestant and I don't believe in them either.

DENNIS

Well, Protestant is a loose synonym for atheist—and I, as an Irishman—and a—

KENNETH

Young man—

DENNIS

Yes?

KENNETH

Have you ever heard Bismarck's solution of the Irish problem?

DENNIS

No. What?

KENNETH

Oh, it's entirely irrelevant.

LEONIE

Please tell us. I adore irrelevancies.

KENNETH

Well, he thought the Irish and the Dutch should exchange countries. The Dutch, he thought, would very soon make a garden out of Ireland, and the Irish would forget to mend the dikes.
[*They laugh.*]

LEONIE

That's not irrelevant—

DENNIS

It is an irrelevance, but pardonable in an adversary losing an argument.

KENNETH

[*To* PAULA.]
Miss Frothingham, you seem very gracious. Will you get me out of this?

PAULA

No, I'm enjoying it.

LEONIE

Whatever you may say, Dennis, it's an exciting time to be alive.

DENNIS
That is because your abnormal situation renders you free of its major excitement—

LEONIE
And what's that, Dennis?

DENNIS
The race with malnutrition.

KENNETH
But that race, Mr.—?

DENNIS
McCarthy.

KENNETH
Is the eternal condition of mankind. Perhaps mankind won't survive the solution of that problem.

WILL
[*With heat.*]
It's easy to sit in this living room—and be smug about the survival of the fittest—especially when you're convinced you're one of the fittest. But there are millions who won't concede you that superiority, Dr. Rice. There are millions who are so outrageously demanding that they actually insist on the right to live! They may demand it one day at the cost of your complacency.

END OF SUMMER

LEONIE

Will! We were just chatting.

WILL

I'm sorry! The next thing Dr. Rice'll be telling us is that war is necessary also—to keep us stimulated—blood-letting for the other fellow.

KENNETH

Well, as a matter of fact, there's something to be said for that too. If you haven't settled on a career yet, Mr. Dexter, may I suggest evangelism?

DENNIS

But Dr. Rice—!

KENNETH

And now, Mrs. Frothingham, before these young people heckle me too effectively, may I escape to my room?

LEONIE

[*Rising.*]
Of course. Though I don't think you need be afraid of their heckling, Doctor. You say things which I've always believed but never dared say.

END OF SUMMER

KENNETH

[*As they walk out.*]
Why not?

LEONIE

I don't know—somehow—I lacked the—the authority. I want to show you your rooms myself.
[*Leaving the room, followed by* RICE.]
I'll be right back, Sam—
[RICE *nods to them and follows her out. As they go out she keeps talking to him.*]
I am giving you my father's rooms—he built the wing especially so that when he wanted to work he'd be away from the rest of the house—you have the sea *and* the garden—
[*They are off. A moment's pause.*]

PAULA

Well, that's a new type for Leonie!

DENNIS

There's something Rasputinish about him. What's he doing in Maine?

WILL

What, for the matter of that, are you and I doing in Maine? We should be in New York, jockeying for position on the bread-line. Let's go to the beach, Dennis. Pep us up for the struggle.

DENNIS
In that surf? It looks angry. I can't face life today.

PAULA
Swim'll do you good.

DENNIS
[*Starting for garden.*]
It's not a swim I want exactly but a float—a vigorous float. Lead me to the pool, Adonais—

WILL
All right.
[*As he starts to follow,* DENNIS, DR. DEXTER, WILL's *father, comes in ushered by* ROBERT. *He is a dusty little man with a bleached yellow Panama hat. He keeps wiping his perspiring face with an old handkerchief. He doesn't hear very well.*]

DENNIS
Ah, the enemy—!
[PAULA *and* SAM *rise.*]

WILL
Hello, dad. You remember Paula?

DEXTER
Yes . . . yes, I do.

WILL
[*Introducing* SAM.]
My father—Mr. Frothingham.

SAM
Very glad to see you.

DEXTER
[*Shaking hands.*]
Thank you.

DENNIS
[*Pointing dramatically at* DEXTER.]
Nevertheless I repeat—the enemy!

PAULA
Dennis!

WILL
Oh, he's used to Dennis!

DEXTER
[*Wipes his forehead.*]
Yes, and besides it was very dusty on the road.

END OF SUMMER

PAULA

Won't you sit down?
[DEXTER *does so, in center chair. The others remain standing.*]

WILL

How long did it take you to drive over, dad?

DEXTER

Let's see—left New Brunswick at two. . . .

WILL

[*Looks at watch.*]
Three and one half hours—pretty good—the old tin Lizzie's got life in her yet.

DEXTER

You young folks having a good time, I suppose?
[*He looks around him absent-mindedly.*]

PAULA

Dennis has been bullying us.

DEXTER

He still talking?
[*Mildly.*]
It's the Irish in him.

END OF SUMMER

DENNIS

[*Nettled.*]
You forgot to say shanty!

DEXTER

[*Surprised.*]
Eh? Why should I say that?

WILL

Dennis is a snob. Wants all his titles.

DENNIS

You misguided children don't realize it—but here—in the guise of this dusty, innocent-seeming man—sits the enemy.

DEXTER

[*Turning as if stung by a fly—cupping his hand to his ear.*]
What? What did he say?

DENNIS

The ultimate enemy, the true begetter of the fatal statistics—Science. You betray us, Paula, by having him in the house; *you* betray us, Will, by acknowledging him as a father.

END OF SUMMER

DEXTER

[*Wiping his forehead.*]
Gosh, it's hot!

SAM

[*Sensing a fight and urging it on—solemnly.*]
Can all this be true, Dr. Dexter?

DEXTER

What be true?

SAM

Dennis's accusation.

DEXTER

I am slightly deaf and McCarthy's presence always fills me with gratitude for that affliction.

DENNIS

It's perfectly obvious. You've heard of technological unemployment. Well, here it sits, embodied in Will's father. Day and night with diabolical ingenuity and cunning he works out devices to un-employ us. All over the world, millions of us are being starved and broken on the altar of Science. We Catholics understand that. We Catholics repudiate the new Moloch that has us by the throat.

END OF SUMMER

WILL

Do you want us to sit in mediæval taverns with Chesterton and drink beer?

[DEXTER *turns to* DENNIS; *as if emerging suddenly from an absent-minded daze, he speaks with great authority, casually but with clarity and precision.*]

DEXTER

The fact is, my voluble young friend, I am not the Moloch who is destroying you but that you and the hordes of the imprecise and the vaguely trained—are destroying me! I have, you will probably be pleased to learn, just lost my job. I have been interrupted in my work. And why? Because I am successful. Because I have found what, with infinite patience and concentration, I have been seeking to discover. From the elusive and the indeterminate and the invisible, I have crystallized a principle which is visible and tangible and—predictable. From the illimitable icebergs of the unknown I have chipped off a fragment of knowledge, a truth which so-called practical men may put to a use which will make some of your numbers unnecessary in the workaday world. Well—what of it, I say?—who decrees that you shall be supported? Of what importance are your lives and your futures and your meandering aspirations compared to the firmness and the beauty and the cohesion of the principles I seek, the truth I seek? None—none whatever! Whether you prattle on an empty stomach or whether you prattle on a full stomach can make no difference to anybody that I can see.

[*To* PAULA *abruptly, rising.*]

And now, young woman, as I have been invited here to spend the night, I'd like to see my room!

PAULA

[*Crossing to him.*]

Certainly! Come with me. I'll have Robert show you your room.

[*They go to door back. She calls.*]

Robert!

[ROBERT *enters.*]

Will you take Dr. Dexter to his room?

[DEXTER *follows* ROBERT *out.*]

SAM

Gosh! I thought he was deaf!

WILL

He can hear when he wants to!

[*To* DENNIS.]

Now will you be good!

DENNIS
I'm sorry—I didn't know he'd lost his job or I wouldn't have . . .

WILL
Oh, that's all right. Well, Dennis, how does it feel to be superfluous?

DENNIS
[*Sourly.*]
The man's childish!
[*He goes out, door right through garden.*]

PAULA
Isn't he marvelous? Don't you love Will's father?

SAM
Crazy about him. He's swell.

WILL
He's a pretty good feller. He seems absent-minded but actually he's extremely present-minded. If you'll excuse me, I'm going out to soothe Dennis.
[*He follows* DENNIS *out.*]
[*A pause.*]

SAM
That young man appears to have sound antecedents.

END OF SUMMER

PAULA

Oh, yes—Will's all right, but—oh, Sam—!

SAM

What?

PAULA

With you gone—I'm terrified for Leonie. I really am! When I think of the foolish marriages Leonie would have made if not for you!

SAM

It's a useful function, but I'm afraid I'll have to give it up!

PAULA

[*With new determination.*]
Sam . . .

SAM

Yes, Paula.

PAULA

If Leonie goes Russian—

SAM

Well?

PAULA

Or if she goes Freudian—?

END OF SUMMER

SAM

In any case you and this boy'll probably be getting married.

PAULA

That's far from settled yet.

SAM

Why?

PAULA

Will's scared.

SAM

Is he?

PAULA

Of getting caught in Leonie's silken web.

SAM

That's sensible of him.
[LEONIE *comes back, half running, breathless.*]

LEONIE

Well! Isn't Dr. Rice attractive?

SAM

[*Rising.*]
Very.

PAULA

[*Rising.*]
And so depressed about himself!
[*She goes out—door right.*]

LEONIE

Isn't it extraordinary, Dr. Rice having achieved the position he has—at his age? He's amazing. And think of it, Sam—not yet forty.

SAM

Anybody under forty is young to me!

LEONIE

How old are you, Sam?

SAM

Forbidden ground, Leonie.

LEONIE

I should know, shouldn't I, but I don't. I know your birthday—I always remember your birthday . . .

SAM

You do indeed!

LEONIE

It's June 14. But I don't know how old you are.

SAM

Knowledge in the right place—ignorance in the right place!

LEONIE

[*Meaning it.*]
You're more attractive and charming than ever.

SAM

You're a great comfort.

LEONIE

It's so nice to see you!

SAM

And you too!
[*He is not entirely comfortable—not as unself-conscious and natural as she is.*]

LEONIE

Sometimes I think Paula should see more of you. I think it would be very good for her. What do you think of her new friends?

SAM

They seem nice.

END OF SUMMER

LEONIE

They're all poor and they're very radical. They look on me—my dear, they have the most extraordinary opinion of me . . .

SAM

What is that?

LEONIE

I'm fascinated by them. They think of me as a hopeless kind of spoiled Bourbon living away in a never-never land—a kind of Marie Antoinette . . .

[*She laughs.*]
It's delicious!

SAM

Is Paula radical too?

LEONIE

I think she's trying to be. She's a strange child.

SAM

How do you mean?

LEONIE

Well, when I was a child I was brought up to care only if people were charming or attractive or . . .

SAM

Well-connected . . .

LEONIE

Yes . . . These kids don't care a hoot about that.

SAM

I think the difference between their generation and ours is that we were romantic and they're realistic.

LEONIE

Is that it?

SAM

I think so.

LEONIE

What makes that?

SAM

Changes in the world—the war—the depression. . . .

LEONIE

What did people blame things on before—the war?

SAM

[*Smiling.*]
Oh, on the tariff and on the Republicans—and on the Democrats! Leonie—

END OF SUMMER

LEONIE

Yes, Sam.

SAM

I—I really have something to tell you.

LEONIE

[*Looks up at him curiously.*]
What?
[*Pause.*]

SAM

I am in love with Selena Bryant. We want to get married.

LEONIE

[*Pause—after a moment.*]
Human nature is funny! Mine is!

SAM

Why?

LEONIE

I know I ought to be delighted to release you. Probably I should have spoken to you about it myself before long—separating. And yet—when you tell me—I feel —a pang. . . .

SAM

That's very sweet of you.

END OF SUMMER

LEONIE

One's so possessive—one doesn't want to give up anything.

SAM

For so many years our marriage has been at its best—a friendship. Need that end?

LEONIE

No, Sam. It needn't. I hope truly that it won't.

SAM

What about Paula?

LEONIE

Did you tell Paula?

SAM

Yes. . . .

LEONIE

Did she . . . ?

SAM

[*Rising.*]
Leonie . . .

LEONIE

[*Pauses.*]
Yes, Sam.

END OF SUMMER

SAM

A little while ago you said—you thought Paula ought to see more of me.

LEONIE

Yes . . . I did. . . .

[*She is quite agitated suddenly. The thought has crossed her mind that perhaps* PAULA *has told* SAM *that she would prefer to go with him. This hurts her deeply, not only for the loss of* PAULA *but because, from the bottom of her being, she cannot bear not to be loved.*]

SAM

Don't you think then . . . for a time at least . . .

LEONIE

[*Defeatist in a crisis.*]
Paula doesn't like me!
[*It is a sudden and completely accepted conviction.*]

SAM

Leonie!

LEONIE

She'd rather go with you!

END OF SUMMER

SAM

Not at all—it's only that . . .

LEONIE

I know what Paula thinks of me. . . .

SAM

Paula adores you. It's only that . . .

LEONIE

It's only that what—

SAM

Well, for instance—if you should get married—

LEONIE

What if I did?

SAM

[*Coming to stand close to her left.*]
It would mean a considerable readjustment for Paula—wouldn't it? You can see that. . . .

LEONIE

[*Rising.*]
But it would too with you and Selena.

END OF SUMMER

SAM

[*Taking step toward her.*]
She knows Selena. She admires Selena.

LEONIE

[*Rising and walking down to front of sofa.*]
What makes you think she wouldn't admire—whomever I married?

SAM

[*After a moment, completely serious now.*]
There's another aspect of it which I think for Paula's sake you should consider most carefully.

LEONIE

What aspect?

SAM

[*Coming down to her.*]
Paula's serious. You know that yourself. She's interested in things. She's not content to be a Sunday-supplement heiress—floating along—she wants to do things. Selena's a working woman. Selena can help her.

LEONIE

I know. I'm useless.

SAM

I think you ought to be unselfish about this.

END OF SUMMER

LEONIE
Paula can do what she likes, of course. If she doesn't love me . . .

SAM
Of course she loves you.

LEONIE
If she prefers to live with you and Selena I shan't stand in her way.
> [*Her martyrish resignation irritates* SAM *profoundly. He feels that really* LEONIE *should not be allowed to get away with it.*]

SAM
You're so vain, Leonie.

LEONIE
[*Refusing to argue.*]
I'm sorry.
> [*This makes it worse.* SAM *goes deeper.*]

SAM
After all, you're Paula's mother. Can't you look at her problem—objectively?

END OF SUMMER

LEONIE

Where my emotions are involved I'm afraid I never know what words like that mean.

[*He blunders in worse, farther than he really means to go.*]

SAM

[*Flatly.*]

Well, this sort of thing isn't good for Paula.

LEONIE

[*Very cold, very hurt.*]

What sort of thing?

[*A moment's pause. He is annoyed with himself at the ineptitude of his approach.*]

Be perfectly frank. You can be with me. What sort of thing?

SAM

Well—Leonie—

[*With a kind of desperate bluntness.*]

You've made a career of flirtation. Obviously Paula isn't going to. You know you and Paula belong to different worlds.

[*With some heat.*]

And the reason Paula is the way she is is because she lives in an atmosphere of perpetual conflict.

END OF SUMMER

LEONIE

Conflict? Paula?

SAM

With herself. About you.

LEONIE

[*Rising.*]
That's too subtle for me, I'm afraid.

SAM

Paula's unaware of it herself.

LEONIE

Where did you acquire this amazing psychological insight? You never used to have it. Of course! From Selena. Of course!

SAM

I've never discussed this with Selena.

LEONIE

No?

SAM

She's told me she'd be happy to have Paula but . . .

END OF SUMMER

LEONIE
That's extremely generous of her—to offer without discussion. . . .

SAM
[*She has him there; he loses his temper.*]
It's impossible for you to consider anything without being personal.

LEONIE
I am afraid it is. I don't live on this wonderful, rarefied, intellectual plane inhabited by Selena and yourself—and where you want to take Paula. I'm sorry if I've made Paula serious, I'm sorry she's in a perpetual conflict about me. I'm sorry I've let her in for—this sort of thing! I'm sorry!
[*She is on the verge of tears. She runs out.*]

SAM
Leonie . . . !
[*He follows her to door back, calling.*]
Leonie!
[*But it is too late. She is gone. He turns back into room.*]
Damn!
[PAULA *comes in—from beach, door right.*]

END OF SUMMER

PAULA

Where's Leonie?

SAM

She just went upstairs.

PAULA

I've been showing Dr. Rice our rock-bound coast.

SAM

What's he like?

PAULA

Hard to say. He's almost too sympathetic. At the same time—

SAM

What?

PAULA

At the same time—he is inscrutable! I can't tell whether I like him or dislike him. You say Selena knows him. What does she say about him?

SAM

Selena isn't crazy about him.

PAULA

Why not?

END OF SUMMER

SAM

Brilliant charlatan, she says—also a charmer.

PAULA

I gather that, and I resent him. How'd you come out with Leonie?

SAM

I've made a mess of it. I'm a fool!

PAULA

My going with you, you mean?

SAM

Yes.

PAULA

Sam . . .

SAM

Yes?

PAULA

Will you mind very much . . .

SAM

What?

PAULA

If I don't go with Selena and you?

END OF SUMMER

SAM

But I thought you said—and especially if she marries somebody—

PAULA

[*Slowly.*]
That's just what I'm thinking of—

SAM

What's happened?

PAULA

There's no way out of it, Sam—I've got to stay.

SAM

But why?

PAULA

[*Simply, looking up at him.*]
Somebody's got to look after Leonie. . . .
[KENNETH *enters.*]

KENNETH

My first glimpse of Maine. A masculine Riviera.

PAULA

It's mild now. If you want to see it really virile—come in the late fall.

END OF SUMMER

KENNETH

You've only to crook your little finger. I'll be glad to look at more of Maine whenever you have the time.
[*Sits, facing her.*]

PAULA

Of course. Tomorrow?

KENNETH

Yes. Tomorrow.
[*To* SAM.]
You know, from Mrs. Frothingham's description—
[*Looking back at* PAULA, *intently.*]
I never could have imagined her. Not remotely.
[ROBERT *enters.*]

SAM

What is it, Robert?

ROBERT

Mrs. Frothingham would like to see Dr. Rice in her study.

KENNETH

[*Rising.*]
Oh, thank you.
[*He walks to door back.*]
Excuse me.

END OF SUMMER

[*He goes upstairs.* PAULA *and* SAM *have continued looking front. As* KENNETH *starts upstairs they slowly turn and look at one another. The same thought has crossed both their minds—they both find themselves looking suddenly into a new and dubious vista.*]

Curtain

ACT TWO

ACT TWO

Scene I

Scene: *The same.*

Time: *Midsummer—late afternoon.*

At Rise: KENNETH *is at a bridge table working out a chess problem. He hears voices and footsteps approaching. Gets up, unhurried, and looks off into garden. Sees* BORIS *and* LEONIE *approaching. As they come in he strolls off—they do not see him.* LEONIE'S *arms are full of flowers. She is looking for* KENNETH. COUNT MIRSKY *follows her in.*

COUNT MIRSKY, *a Russian, is very good-looking, mongoloid about the eyes. His English is beautiful, with a slight and attractive accent. He is tense, jittery —a mass of jangled nerves—his fingers tremble as he lights one cigarette after another. He is very pale— his pallor accentuated by a dark scarf he wears around his neck.*

END OF SUMMER

BORIS

[*Stopping center.*]
It appears he is not here either.

LEONIE

He? Who?
[*Crossing to table behind sofa to put some flowers in vase.*]

BORIS

When you're in the garden with me you think—perhaps he is in the house. When you are in the house you think perhaps he is in the garden.

LEONIE

Boris, darling, you have the odd habit of referring to mysterious characters without giving me any hint who they are. Is that Russian symbolism? There will be a long silence; then you will say: He would not approve, or they can't hear us. It's a bit mystifying.

BORIS

[*Crossing to stand near her.*]
You know who I mean.

LEONIE

[*Going to table right to put flowers in vase.*]
Really, you flatter me. I'm not a mystic, you know,

END OF SUMMER

Boris. I'm a simple extrovert. When you say "he," why can't it refer to someone definite—and if possible to someone I know.

BORIS
[*Crossing to back of table, facing her across it.*]
You know him, all right.

LEONIE
There you go again! *Really*, Boris!

BORIS
[*Moving closer to her around table.*]
You've been divorced now for several weeks. You're free. We were only waiting for you to be free—

LEONIE
[*Moving away, sitting in chair, right.*]
Now that I am free you want to coerce me. It's a bit unreasonable, don't you think?
[BORIS *walks to end of window-seat and sits.*]
[*Enter* KENNETH, *door back.*]

KENNETH

[*Strolling across stage toward* LEONIE.]
Hello, Leonie. Count Mirsky—

LEONIE

Kenneth—I haven't seen you all day.

KENNETH

I've been in my room slaving away at a scientific paper.

LEONIE

My house hums with creative activity. I love it. It gives me a sense of vicarious importance. What's your paper on?

KENNETH

Shadow-neurosis.

LEONIE

Shadow-neurosis. How marvelous! What does it mean?

KENNETH

[*Looking at* BORIS.]
It is a sensation of non-existence.

LEONIE

Is it common?

END OF SUMMER

KENNETH

Quite. The victim knows that he exists and yet he feels that he does not!

LEONIE

In a curious way I can imagine a sensation like that—do you know I actually can. Isn't it amusing?

BORIS

The doctor is so eloquent. Once he describes a sensation it becomes very easy to feel it.

LEONIE

That's an entrancing gift. Why are you so antagonistic to Kenneth? He wants to help you but you won't let him. I asked him here to help you.

KENNETH

[*To* BORIS.]
Your skepticism about this particular disease is interesting, Count Mirsky, because, as it happens, you suffer from it.

BORIS

[*Bearing down on* KENNETH.]
Has it ever occurred to you that you are a wasted novelist?

END OF SUMMER

KENNETH

Though I have not mentioned you in my article I have described you.

LEONIE

[*Rising and crossing left to table behind sofa.*]
You should be flattered, Boris.

BORIS

I am!

LEONIE

Another case history! I've been reading some of Kenneth's scientific text-books. Most fascinating form of biography. Who was that wonderful fellow who did such odd things—Mr. X.? You'd never think you could get so interested in anonymous people. I'd have given anything to meet Mr. X.—though I must say I'd feel a bit nervous about having him in the house.

KENNETH

How is your book getting along, Count Mirsky?

BORIS

Very well. Oh—so—

KENNETH
Far along in it?

BORIS
Quite.

LEONIE
I'm crazy to see it. He's dedicating it to me but he hasn't let me see a word of it!

KENNETH
For a very good reason.

LEONIE
What do you mean?

KENNETH
Because there is no book. There never has been a book.

LEONIE
[*She lets flowers drop.*]
Kenneth!

KENNETH
Isn't that true, Count Mirsky?

BORIS
It is not!

END OF SUMMER

KENNETH
Then why don't you let us see a bit of it?

LEONIE
Oh, do! At least the dedication page.

KENNETH
A chapter—

BORIS
Because it isn't finished yet.

LEONIE
Well, it doesn't have to be finished. We know the end, don't we? The end belongs to the world.

KENNETH
Let us see it, Count.

BORIS
I can't.

KENNETH
What are you calling the book?

BORIS
I haven't decided yet.

END OF SUMMER

KENNETH

May I suggest a title to you—?

LEONIE

Oh, do! What shall we call it, Kenneth?

KENNETH

"The Memoirs of a Boy Who Wanted to Murder His Father."

LEONIE

What!

BORIS

[*Gripping arms of chair.*]

I am not a hysterical woman, Doctor—and I'm not your patient!

LEONIE

But Kenneth—Boris worshipped his father.

KENNETH

No, he hated him. He hated him when he was alive and he hates him still. He grew up under the overwhelming shadow of this world-genius whom, in spite of an immense desire to emulate and even to surpass— he felt he could never emulate and never surpass—nor even equal— Did you worship your father, Count Mirsky?

END OF SUMMER

BORIS

It's true! I hated him!

LEONIE

Boris!

BORIS

I hated him!

KENNETH

Now you can let us see the book, can't you—now that we know the point of view—just a bit of it?

LEONIE

I'm more crazy than ever to see it now. I can tell you a little secret now, Boris. I was afraid—I was rather afraid—that your book would be a little like one of those statues of an ancestor in a frock-coat. Now it sounds really exciting. You hated him. But how perfectly marvelous! I can't wait to see it now. Do run up to your study and bring it down, Boris—do!

BORIS

No.

LEONIE

That's very unpleasant of you.

END OF SUMMER

BORIS

You might as well know it then. There isn't any book. There never will be. Not by me.

LEONIE

But I don't understand—every day—in your room working—all these months!

BORIS

[*Facing her.*]
One wants privacy! Possibly you can't realize that. You who always have to have a house full of people.

LEONIE

[*Goes back to flowers at table.*]
Boris!

KENNETH

[*Rising.*]
Why don't you write the book anyway, Count Mirsky? There is a vogue these days for vituperative biography.

BORIS

I am not interested in the vogue.

KENNETH

We are quite used nowadays to children who dislike their fathers. The public—

END OF SUMMER

BORIS

To titillate the public would not compensate me for forcing myself to recall the atmosphere of saintly sadism in which my childhood was spent—I can still smell that living room, I can still smell those stinking, sexless pilgrims who used to come from all over the world to get my saintly father's blessing. I used to sit with my mother in a room no bigger than a closet to get away from the odor of that nauseating humanitarianism. There was no privacy in the Villa Mirskovitch. Oh, no—it was a Mecca—do you understand—a Mecca!

KENNETH

Yes, I think I understand.

BORIS

Well, I have been paying the haloed one back. I have been getting privacy at his expense at last.

LEONIE

Why have you never told me before that you felt this way about your father?

BORIS

I never said anything about him. It was you who did the talking. You always raved about the great man with that characteristic American enthusiasm for what you don't know.

LEONIE

Nevertheless, the world recognizes your father as a great man. The books are there to prove it. There they are. You can't write books like that without greatness—no matter what you say. You are a petulant child. Your father was a great man.

BORIS

It makes no difference how great he was—those pilgrims stank!

[LEONIE *turns away.*]

KENNETH

I suggest that to write that book, even if no one ever sees the manuscript but you, might amuse you—a kind of revenge which, when you were a boy, you were in no position to take.

BORIS

Are you trying to cure me, Doctor? Please don't trouble. I don't need your particular species of professionalism. I do not need any help from you.

[*He goes to door back, turns to* LEONIE. LEONIE *looks bewilderedly at* KENNETH. BORIS *goes out.*]

END OF SUMMER

LEONIE

How did you know? You're uncanny!

KENNETH

All in the day's work.

LEONIE

Why is it I always get myself involved with men weaker than myself? I certainly am no tower of strength.

KENNETH

Possibly not—but you are generous and impulsive. You have a tendency to accept people at the best of their own valuation.

LEONIE

I want to help them. I do help them. After they get used to my help, after they get to count on my help, I get impatient with them. Why, I ask myself, can't people help themselves?

KENNETH

And very natural.

LEONIE

I seem to attract people like that!

END OF SUMMER

KENNETH

Leonie—you are the last woman on earth Count Mirsky should marry. He would only transfer his hatred of his father to you.

LEONIE

I don't think I understand you, Kenneth—really I don't—and I do so want to understand things.

KENNETH

Well—your charm, your gaiety, your position, your wealth, your beauty—these would oppress him. Again, he cannot be himself.—Or, if he is himself, it is to reveal his nonentity, his inferiority—again the secondary rôle—Leonie Frothingham's husband—the son of Count Mirsky—the husband of Leonie Frothingham. Again the shadow—again, eternally and always—nonexistence. Poor fellow.

[*Pause.*]

LEONIE

I'm so grateful to you, Kenneth.

KENNETH

Nonsense. You mustn't be grateful to me because I —exercise my profession.

END OF SUMMER

LEONIE

I want to express my gratitude—in some tangible form. I've been thinking of nothing else lately. I can't sleep for thinking of it.

KENNETH

Well, if it gives you insomnia, you'd better tell me about it.

LEONIE

I want to make it possible for you to realize your ambition.

KENNETH

Ambition? What ambition?

LEONIE

Ah! You've forgotten, haven't you? But you let it slip out one day—you pump me professionally—but I do the same to you—non-professionally.

KENNETH

You terrify me!

LEONIE

That night last winter when we went to dinner in that little restaurant where you go with your doctor friends . . . you told me your dream.

END OF SUMMER

KENNETH

My censor must have been napping.

LEONIE

He was. Or she was. What sex is your censor?

KENNETH

That's none of your business.

LEONIE

I'm sorry.

KENNETH

Which of my dreams was I so reckless as to reveal to you?

LEONIE

To have a sanatorium of your own one day—so you can carry out your own ideas of curing patients.

KENNETH

Oh, that! Out of the question.

LEONIE

Why?

KENNETH

To do it on the scale I visualize, would cost more than I'm ever likely to save out of my practice.

LEONIE
I'll give you the sanatorium. I've never given anyone anything like that before. What fun!

KENNETH
Will I find it all wrapped up in silver foil on Christmas morning?

LEONIE
Yes. You will! You will! We'll have a suite in it for Mr. X.—for all your anonymous friends—we'll entertain the whole alphabet!

KENNETH
You see, Leonie!

LEONIE
What do you mean? I thought you'd be—

KENNETH
Of course, it's terribly generous of you. I'm deeply touched. But . . .

LEONIE
But . . . ?

KENNETH
I'm a stranger to you.

END OF SUMMER

LEONIE

Kenneth!

KENNETH

Outside of my professional relation—such as I have with scores of patients—little more than that.

LEONIE

I thought—

KENNETH

And yet you are willing to back me in a venture that would cost a sizeable fortune—just on that. Leonie! Leonie!

LEONIE

It would be the best investment I've ever made. Paula's always telling me I have no social consciousness. Well, this would be.—It would keep me from feeling so useless. I do feel useless, Kenneth. Please!

KENNETH

I'm sorry. I couldn't hear of it. Of course, it's out of the question.

LEONIE

It isn't. I can afford it. Why shouldn't I? It would be helping so many people—you have no right to refuse. It's selfish of you to refuse.

END OF SUMMER

KENNETH

I distrust impulsive altruism. You will forgive me, Leonie, but it may often do harm.

LEONIE

How do you mean, Kenneth?

KENNETH

I gather you are about to endow a radical magazine for the *boys*—

LEONIE

Will and Dennis! I thought it would be nice to give them something to do!

KENNETH

Yes. You are prepared to back them in a publication which, if it attained any influence, would undermine the system which makes you and people like you possible.

LEONIE

But it never occurred to me anyone would read it.

KENNETH

There is a deplorably high literacy in this country. Unfortunately it is much easier to learn to read than it is to learn to think.

LEONIE

Well, if you don't think it's a good idea, Kenneth, I won't do it. But this sanatorium is different.

KENNETH

Why?

LEONIE

Because, if you must know it, it would be helping you—and that means everything in the world to me. There, I've said it. It's true! Kenneth—are you terrified?

KENNETH

You adorable child!

LEONIE

It's extraordinary, Kenneth—but you are the first strong man who's ever come into my life—

[*Enter* PAULA, DENNIS, WILL, *door back.*]

Oh, I'm very glad to see you! Will! Hullo, Dennis. You all know Dr. Rice. Mr. Dexter, Mr. McCarthy. Sit down, everybody. Well, children, how is New York?

[DENNIS *crosses down front of them to chair left by sofa and sits.*]

WILL

Stifling, thank you.

LEONIE

Any luck yet?

WILL

I am available, but New York is dead to its chief opportunity.

LEONIE

Then you can stay here for a bit. You can both stay here.

DENNIS

That was all right when we were in college, Mrs. Frothingham. Can't do it now.

LEONIE

Oh, you're working. I'm so glad!

DENNIS

I beg your pardon. Did you say working?

LEONIE

Well, then! I don't see why you can't stay here and take a holiday.

WILL

From what?

END OF SUMMER

LEONIE

Since none of you are doing anything in town, you might as well stay here and do nothing and be comfortable.

DENNIS

Yes, but it's an ethical question. When we're in New York doing nothing, we belong to the most respectable vested group going! The unemployed. As such we have a status, position, authority. But if we stay here doing nothing—what are we? Low-down parasites.

KENNETH

No jobs about anywhere, eh?

WILL

Extinct commodity.

DENNIS

I did pretty well last week.

LEONIE

Really?

DENNIS

I was rejected by seven newspapers—including the *Bronx Home News* and the *Yonkers Herald*—six magazines and trade papers—a total of twenty-eight rejections in all, representing a net gain over the previous week of seven solid rejections. I submit to you, gentlemen, that's progress—pass the cigars, Will.

LEONIE
Couldn't you stay here and be rejected by mail?

DENNIS
Doesn't give you that same feeling somehow—that good, rich, dark-brown sensation of not being wanted!

LEONIE
You know, Kenneth, in a curious way, Dennis reminds me a bit of Mr. X.

DENNIS
And who's X.?

LEONIE
A sporting acquaintance.

DENNIS
There's one thing I'd like to ask Dr. Rice. . . . Do you mind?

KENNETH
At your service.

DENNIS
[*Turning chair and facing* KENNETH *upstage.*]

END OF SUMMER

In the psychoanalytic hierarchy Freud is the god, isn't he?

KENNETH

Of one sect, yes.

DENNIS

Well, the original sect—

KENNETH

Yes. . . .

DENNIS

Now, every psychoanalyst has to have himself analyzed. That's true, isn't it, Doctor?

KENNETH

Generally speaking—yes.

DENNIS

As I understand it, the highest prices go to those nearest the Master himself.

KENNETH

This boy is irreverent . . .

DENNIS

I know whereof I speak. I prepared an article on the subject for *Fortune*.

END OF SUMMER

WILL
Rejection number three hundred.

DENNIS
I am afraid, Will, that you are a success worshipper!

LEONIE
Dennis is an *enfant terrible,* and he exhausts himself keeping it up!

DENNIS
I have examined the racket with a microscopic patience and this I find to be true: at the top of the hierarchy is the Great Pan Sexualist of Vienna. To be an orthodox and accepted Freudian, you must have been analyzed by another of the same. Now, what I am burning to know is this: Who analyzed Sig Freud himself? Whom does he tell his repressions to? Why, the poor guy must be as lonely as hell!

LEONIE
What would you do with him, Kenneth? He has no repressions whatever!

KENNETH
He needs some badly.

END OF SUMMER

LEONIE

I wonder what Dennis would confess to his psychoanalyst that he isn't always shouting to the world?

DENNIS

I'd make the psychoanalyst talk.
[*To* KENNETH. *Beckoning.*]
Tell me, Doctor, what did you dream last night?

KENNETH

[*Behind his cupped hand.*]
Not in public.

DENNIS

[*Rises and crosses straight right.*]
You see—he's repressed! I tell you these psychoanalysts are repressed. They've got nobody to talk to! I'm going swimming. It's pathetic!
[*He goes out.*]

LEONIE

I'm going too. He makes me laugh. How about you, Kenneth?

KENNETH

Oh, I'll watch.

LEONIE

[*To others.*]
Come along with us. There's plenty of time for a swim before dinner.

END OF SUMMER

[KENNETH *starts out with* LEONIE—*stops on the way.*]

KENNETH

I suppose you and your Irish friend edited the comic paper at college?

WILL

No, we edited the serious paper.

KENNETH

Just the same it must have been very funny.
[*He goes out after* LEONIE.]

WILL

Don't think that feller likes me much.

PAULA

You're psychic.

WILL

Well, for the matter of that I'm not crazy about him either.

PAULA

Don't bother about him. Concentrate on me!

WILL

How are you, darling?

END OF SUMMER

PAULA

Missed you.

WILL

[*Pulls her to sofa and sits with her.* PAULA *left end sofa.*]
And I you. Pretty lousy in town without you.

PAULA

Oh, poor darling!

WILL

Although my star is rising. I did some book-reviews for the New York *Times* and the *New Masses*.

PAULA

What a gamut!

WILL

I made, in fact, a total of eleven dollars. The student most likely to succeed in the first four months since graduation has made eleven dollars.

PAULA

Wonderful!

WILL

My classmates were certainly clairvoyant. As a matter of fact, I shouldn't have told you. Now I'll be tortured thinking you're after me for my money.

PAULA

You'll never know!

WILL

[*Putting arm around her shoulders and drawing her to him.*]
What've you been doing?

PAULA

Lying in the sun mostly.

WILL

Poor little Ritz girl.

PAULA

Wondering what you do every night.

WILL

Forty-second Street Library mostly. Great fun! Voluptuary atmosphere!

PAULA

Is your life altogether so austere?

WILL

Well, frankly, no. Not altogether.

END OF SUMMER

PAULA

Cad!

WILL

What do you expect?

PAULA

Loyalty.

WILL

I am loyal. But you go around all day job-hunting. You find you're not wanted. It's reassuring after that to find a shoulder to lean on, sort of haven where you *are* wanted. Even the public library closes at ten. You have to go somewhere. If I'm ever Mayor of New York, I'll have the public libraries kept open all night . . . the flop-houses of the intellectuals!

PAULA

Is it anyone special . . . ?

WILL

Just a generalized shoulder.

PAULA

Well, you're going to have a special one from now on—mine! You know, the way you're avoiding the issue is all nonsense.

END OF SUMMER

WILL

You mean my gallant fight against you?

PAULA

I've decided that you are conventional and bourgeois. You're money-ridden.

WILL

Eleven dollars. They say a big income makes you conservative.

PAULA

I don't mean your money. I mean—my money. It's childish to let an artificial barrier like that stand between us. It's also childish to ignore it.

WILL

[*Rising.*]
I don't ignore it. That's what worries me. I count on it. Already I find myself counting on it. I can't help it. Sitting and waiting in an office for some bigwig who won't see me or for some underling who won't see me I think: "Why the Hell should I wait all day for this stuffed shirt?" I don't wait. Is it because of you I feel in a special category? Do I count on your money? Is that why I don't wait as long as the other fellow? There's one consolation: the other fellow doesn't get the job either. But the point is disquieting!

END OF SUMMER

PAULA

What a Puritan you are!

WILL

[*Sitting beside her again.*]
Will I become an appendage to you—like your mother's men?

PAULA

You're bound to—money or no money.

WILL

[*Taking her into his arms.*]
I suppose I might as well go on the larger dole—

PAULA

What?

WILL

Once you are paid merely for existing—you are on the dole. I rather hoped, you know—

PAULA

What?

WILL

It's extraordinary the difference in one's thinking when you're in college and when you're out—

PAULA

How do you mean?

WILL

Well, when I was in college, my interest in the—"movement"—was really impersonal. I imagined myself giving my energies to the poor and the downtrodden in my spare time. I didn't really believe I'd be one of the poor and downtrodden myself. In my heart of hearts I was sure I'd break through the iron law of Dennis's statistics and land a job somewhere. But I can't—and it's given a tremendous jolt to my self-esteem.

PAULA

But you'll come through. I'm sure of it. I wish you could learn to look at my money as a means rather than an end.

WILL

I'd rather use my own.

PAULA

You're proud.

WILL

I am.

PAULA

It's humiliating but I'm afraid I've got to ask you to marry me, Will.

END OF SUMMER

WILL

It's humiliating but considering my feelings I see no way out of accepting you.

PAULA

You submit?

WILL

[*Kisses her hand.*]
I submit.

PAULA

After a hard campaign—victory!

WILL

You *are* a darling.

PAULA

[*Getting up and crossing to center.*]
I can't tell you what a relief it'll be to get away from this house.

WILL

Why?

PAULA

I don't know. It's getting very complicated.

WILL

Leonie?

END OF SUMMER

PAULA

And Boris. *And* Dr. Rice. Funny thing how that man . . .

WILL

What?

PAULA

Makes you insecure somehow.

WILL

Supposed to do just the opposite.

PAULA

He answers every question—and yet he's secretive. I've never met a man who—who—

WILL

Who what?

PAULA

Really, I can't stand Dr. Rice.

WILL

I believe he fascinates you.

PAULA

He does. I don't deny that. And I can't tell you how I resent it. Isn't it silly?

[*The old lady* WYLER *in a wheel chair is propelled*

in by a nurse. The old lady is much wasted since the preceding summer; she is touched with mortality.]
Granny!

MRS. WYLER

Paula! How are you, my dear?

PAULA

I came up to see you before, but you were asleep.

MRS. WYLER

Nurse told me.
[*Exit* NURSE, *door left.*]

PAULA

You remember Will?

WILL

How do you do, Mrs. Wyler?

MRS. WYLER

Of course. How do you do, young man?

PAULA

Well, this is quite an adventure for you, isn't it, Granny?

END OF SUMMER

MRS. WYLER

You're the boy who was always so curious about my youth.

WILL

Yes.

MRS. WYLER

I've forgotten most of it. Now I just live from day to day. The past is just this morning.

[*A moment's pause.*]

And I don't always remember that very well. Aren't there insects who live only one day? The morning is their youth and the afternoon their middle age. . . .

PAULA

You don't seem yourself today. Not as cheerful as usual.

MRS. WYLER

Can't I have my moods, Paula? I am pleased to be reflective today. People are always sending me funny books to read. I've been reading one and it depressed me.

PAULA

Well, I'll tell you something to cheer you up, Granny —Will and I are going to be married.

MRS. WYLER

Have you told your mother?

PAULA

Not yet. It's a secret.
[*Enter* KENNETH.]

KENNETH

Well, Mrs. Wyler! Wanderlust today?

MRS. WYLER

Yes! Wanderlust!

KENNETH

Paula, if you're not swimming, what about our walk, and our daily argument?

MRS. WYLER

What argument?

KENNETH

Paula is interested in my subject. She hovers between skepticism and fascination.

PAULA

No chance to hover today, Kenneth. Will's improving his tennis. Sorry.

END OF SUMMER

KENNETH

So am I.

MRS. WYLER

I've a surprise for you, Paula.

PAULA

What?

MRS. WYLER

Your father's coming.

PAULA

No!

MRS. WYLER

Yes.

PAULA

But how—! How do you know?

MRS. WYLER

Because I've sent for him, and he wired me he's coming. He's driving from Blue Hill. He should be here now.

PAULA

That's too—! Oh, Granny, that's marvelous! Will, let's drive out to meet him, shall we? Does Mother know?

MRS. WYLER

I only had Sam's wire an hour ago.

END OF SUMMER

PAULA

Granny, you're an angel.

MRS. WYLER

Not quite yet. Don't hurry me, child.

PAULA

Come on, Will.
[*Exit* PAULA *and* WILL.]

MRS. WYLER

I can see you are interested in Paula. You are, aren't you, Dr. Rice?

KENNETH

Yes. She's an extraordinary child. Adores her father, doesn't she?

MRS. WYLER

How would you cure that, Doctor?

KENNETH

It's quite healthy.

MRS. WYLER

Really? I was hoping for something juicy in the way of interpretation.

END OF SUMMER

KENNETH

Sorry!

MRS. WYLER

What an interesting profession yours is, Dr. Rice.

KENNETH

Why particularly?

MRS. WYLER

Your province is the soul. Strange region.

KENNETH

People's souls, I find are, on the whole, infinitely more interesting than their bodies. I have been a general practitioner and I know.

MRS. WYLER

These young people—don't they frighten you?

KENNETH

Frighten!

MRS. WYLER

They are so radical—prepared to throw everything overboard—every tradition—

KENNETH

Paula's friends have nothing to lose, any change would be—in the nature of velvet for them.

MRS. WYLER
What do you think of Will?

KENNETH
I'm afraid I've formed no strongly defined opinion on Will.

MRS. WYLER
Oh, I see— That is a comment in itself.

KENNETH
He's nondescript.

MRS. WYLER
Do you mean to point that out to Paula?

KENNETH
I don't think so. That won't be necessary.

MRS. WYLER
Why not?

KENNETH
Blood will tell.

MRS. WYLER
That's very gracious of you, Doctor.
[*Pause.*]
And what do you think of Leonie?

END OF SUMMER

KENNETH

Very endearing—and very impulsive.

MRS. WYLER

For example—I mean of the latter—

KENNETH

She offered to build me a sanatorium—a fully equipped modern sanatorium.

MRS. WYLER

Did she? Convenient for you.

KENNETH

Except that I refused.

MRS. WYLER

Wasn't that quixotic?

KENNETH

Not necessarily.
[PAULA *and* SAM *enter, door back.*]

PAULA

Here he is!

MRS. WYLER

Sam!

END OF SUMMER

SAM

Louise!

PAULA

He wouldn't come if I'd ask him. He said so shamelessly. You know Dr. Rice?

SAM

Of course.

KENNETH

Excuse me.
[KENNETH *goes out.*]

SAM

Well, Louise!

MRS. WYLER

Hello, Sam.
[SAM *kisses her.*]

SAM

How's she behaving?

PAULA

Incorrigible. Dr. Prentiss tells her to rest in her room. You see how she obeys him. She'll obey you though.

SAM

Well, I'll sneak her away from Dr. Prentiss and take her abroad.

MRS. WYLER

I want to go to Ethiopia. Run along, dear. I want to talk to Sam.

PAULA

Keep him here, Granny. Pretend you're not feeling well.

MRS. WYLER

I'll try.
[*Exit* PAULA *door back.*]
Well, Sam—

SAM

I got your wire last night. Here I am.

MRS. WYLER

It's nice of you.

SAM

Oh, now, Louise. You know you're the love of my life.

MRS. WYLER

Yes, Sam, I know—but how is Selena?

SAM

Flourishing.

END OF SUMMER

MRS. WYLER

You're all right then?

SAM

Unbelievably.

MRS. WYLER

I knew you would be.

SAM

And you?

MRS. WYLER

I'm dying, Sam.

SAM

Not you—

MRS. WYLER

Don't contradict me. Besides, I'm rather looking forward to it.

SAM

Is Dr. Prentiss—?

MRS. WYLER

Dr. Prentiss soft-soaps me. I let him. It relieves his mind. But that's why I've sent for you.

SAM

You know, my dear—

END OF SUMMER

MRS. WYLER

Yes, Sam. I know I can count on you. I'm dying. And I'm dying alone. I have to talk to somebody. You're the only one.

SAM

Is anything worrying you?

MRS. WYLER

Plenty.

SAM

What, dear?

MRS. WYLER

The future. Not my own. That's fixed or soon will be. But Leonie's—Paula's—

SAM

Aren't they all right?

MRS. WYLER

I am surrounded by aliens. The house is full of strangers. That Russian upstairs; this doctor.

SAM

Rice? Are you worried about him?

END OF SUMMER

MRS. WYLER

What is he after? What does he want? He told me Leonie offered to build him a sanatorium—

SAM

Did he accept it?

MRS. WYLER

No. He refused. But something tells me he will allow himself to be persuaded.

SAM

I don't think Rice is a bad feller really. Seems pretty sensible. Are you worried about this boy— Dexter, and Paula?

MRS. WYLER

Not in the same way. I like the boy. But Paula— I'm worried about what the money'll do to her. We know what it's done to Leonie. You know, Sam, in spite of all her romantic dreams Leonie has a kind of integrity. But I often wonder if she's ever been really happy.

SAM

Oh, now, Louise, this pessimism's unlike you—

MRS. WYLER

This money we've built our lives on—it used to

symbolize security—but there's no security in it any more.

              SAM
Paula'll be all right. I count on Paula.

            MRS. WYLER
In the long run. But that may be too late. One can't let go of everything, Sam. It isn't in nature. That's why I've asked you to come. I want you to remain as executor under my will.

              SAM
Well, I only resigned because—since I'm no longer married to Leonie—

            MRS. WYLER
What has that got to do with it?

              SAM
All right.

            MRS. WYLER
Promise?

              SAM
Certainly.

            MRS. WYLER
I feel something dark ahead, a terror—

END OF SUMMER

SAM

Now, now, you've been brooding.

MRS. WYLER

Outside of you—Will is the soundest person I'll leave behind me, the healthiest—but in him too I feel a recklessness that's just kept in—I see a vista of the unknown—to us the unknown was the West, land—physical hardship—but he's hard and bitter underneath his jocularity—he isn't sure, he says, what he is— Once he is sure, what will he do?—I want you to watch him, Sam, for Paula's sake.

SAM

I will.

MRS. WYLER

They're all strange and dark. . . . And this doctor. A soul doctor. We didn't have such things—I am sure that behind all this is a profound and healing truth. But sometimes truths may be perverted, and this particular doctor—how are we to know where his knowledge ends and his pretension begins? Now that I am dying, for the first time in my life I know fear. Death seems easy and simple, Sam—a self-indulgence—but can I afford it?

[*She smiles up at him. He squeezes her hand.*]

END OF SUMMER

SAM

Everything will be all right. Trust me.

MRS. WYLER

I do.
[*A pause.*]
You'll stay the night?

SAM

Of course.

MRS. WYLER

Now I feel better.

SAM

That's right.
[*Pause.*]

MRS. WYLER

I'd like to live till autumn.

SAM

Of course you will. Many autumns.

MRS. WYLER

Heaven forbid. But this autumn. The color—the leaves turn.
[*Looking out window.* SAM *looks too.*]
The expression seems strange. What do they turn to?

SAM

[*Softly, helping her mood.*]
Their mother. The earth.

MRS. WYLER

I'm happy now. I'm at peace.

SAM

[*Puts arm around her and draws her to him.*]
That's better.

MRS. WYLER

[*Smiling up at him.*]
It's very clever of me to have sent for you, Sam. I'm pleased with myself. Now, Sam, let 'em do their worst—

SAM

[*Smiling back at her and patting her hand.*]
Just let 'em . . . !

Curtain

ACT TWO

Scene II

SCENE: *The same.*

Time: A few hours later—before dinner. LEONIE *is standing in doorway looking out.* BORIS *center; he is fatalistically quiet at first.*

BORIS
What it comes to is this then! You're through with me. You want me to go!

LEONIE
I'm no good to you! I can no longer help you.

BORIS
Frustrated altruist!

LEONIE
You hate me!

BORIS
That would be encouraging!

LEONIE
We have nothing more for each other.

BORIS
Less than we had in the beginning!

LEONIE
Less than I thought we had.

BORIS
[*Walking toward her.*]
And the man of science?

LEONIE
What?

BORIS
[*Still bearing down on her.*]
This intricate man of science. You fluctuate so, Leonie.
[*Facing her.*]

LEONIE
Please, Boris. I've failed. Can't we part—beautifully?

BORIS
What do you want to do? Go out on the bay and say farewell before the villagers in a barge drawn by a flock

of swans? Shall we have a little orchestra to play—with the strings sobbing—and the bassoon off key?

LEONIE

You are bitter and cruel. Why? I've tried to help you. Why are you bitter?

BORIS

[*Moving close to her.*]
At least I'm honest. Can you say the same?

LEONIE

[*Breaking away from him.*]
I don't know what you mean by that.

BORIS

[*Getting in front of her.*]
Yes, you do.

LEONIE

You're eating yourself up. You're killing yourself. There's the great lovely world outside and you sit in your room hating—

BORIS

What do you recommend? Cold showers and Swedish massage? What does the man of science prescribe for me?

LEONIE

Why do you hate Kenneth so?

BORIS

I'm jealous, my dear!

LEONIE

Poor Boris. You're beyond a simple emotion like that, aren't you?

BORIS

I envy you, Leonie. All like you.

LEONIE

Do you?

BORIS

I envy all sentimental liars who gratify their desires on high principle. It makes all your diversions an exercise in piety. You're sick of me and want to sleep with the man of science.

[LEONIE *turns away. He seizes her arms and turns her to him.*]

Does this suffice for you? No. It must be that you can no longer help me.

[*Little silent laugh.*]

My sainted father was like that! God!

END OF SUMMER

LEONIE

This is the end, Boris.

BORIS

Of course it is. I tell you this though: Beware of him, Leonie. Beware of him.

LEONIE

Your hatred of Kenneth—like all your hatreds—they're unnatural, frightening. I'm frightened of you.
[*Turning from him.*]

BORIS

[*Crossing before her, closing door so she can't escape.*]
Much better to be frightened of him. You know what I think. What does he think? Does he tell you? Do you know?

LEONIE

Yes, I know.

BORIS

You know what he tells you. This clairvoyant who gets rich profoundly analyzing the transparent.
[*Enter* KENNETH, *door back.*]

KENNETH

Your mother would like to see you, Leonie.

LEONIE
Is she all right?
[BORIS *goes upstage to small table. Gets cigarette.*]

KENNETH
Oh, very chipper. Mr. Frothingham is with her.

LEONIE
She sent for Sam, didn't she? I wonder why.

BORIS
Perhaps she felt the situation too complicated—even for *you,* Dr. Rice.

KENNETH
I don't think so.

BORIS
You are so Olympian, Dr. Rice. Would it be possible to anger you?

KENNETH
Symptoms, my dear Count, never anger me. I study them.

BORIS
Really, you are in a superb position. I quite envy you. One might cut oneself open in front of you—and it would be a symptom. Wouldn't it?

END OF SUMMER

LEONIE

Boris, please—what's the good?

BORIS

[*Crossing slowly to* LEONIE.]
You are quite right, my dear, no good—no good in the world. Give your mother this message for me. Tell her that under the circumstances I shall simplify the situation by withdrawing.

LEONIE

You make me very unhappy, Boris.

BORIS

How agreeable then that you have Dr. Rice here—to resolve your unhappiness.
[*Crosses quickly to table behind sofa and puts out cigarette.*]

LEONIE

[*Following him.*]
Where will you be in case I—in case you—Boris?

BORIS

Don't worry about me. A magazine syndicate has offered me a great deal for *sentimental* reminiscences of my father. Imagine that, sentimental! They have offered me—charming Americanism—a ghost-writer. It will be quaint—one ghost collaborating with another ghost.

[*Raising hand like Greek priest.*]

My blessings, Leonie.

[*Kisses her hand.*]

You have been charming. Dr. Rice—

[*He bows formally. Exit* BORIS.]

LEONIE

Poor Boris—

[*She sinks into a chair, overcome.*]

KENNETH

He's part of the past. You must forget him.

LEONIE

Poor Boris!

KENNETH

You will forget him.

LEONIE

I'll try.

KENNETH

Exorcised!

END OF SUMMER

LEONIE

You know, Kenneth, I feel you are the only one in the world I can count on.

KENNETH

Not me.

LEONIE

Whom else?

KENNETH

Yourself!

LEONIE

Light reed! Fragile! Fragile!

KENNETH

Pliant but unbreakable.

LEONIE

No. Don't think much of myself, Kenneth. Really I don't. My judgment seems to be at fault somehow. Paula thinks so too. She's always lecturing me.
[*Sits right end of sofa.*]

KENNETH

Paula can't abide me.

LEONIE

It's not true!

END OF SUMMER

KENNETH

You know, Leonie, I have an instinct in these matters—so, also, has your daughter.

LEONIE

Don't you like Paula?

KENNETH

I love her. Everyone connected with you.

LEONIE

Kenneth! How dear of you! Of course Paula and I are poles apart. Look at her friends!

KENNETH

Raffish!

LEONIE

[*A little taken aback by this.*]
Oh, do you think so? All of them? Don't you like Will?

KENNETH

Nice enough. Clever in his way. With an eye to the main chance.

LEONIE

Really?

KENNETH
Naturally—penniless boy.

LEONIE
I've always encouraged Paula to be independent. I've never tried to impose my ideals or my standards on her. Have I done wrong to give her her own head this way? She's such a darling, really. She's killing, you know. So superior, so knowing. The other day—the other day, Kenneth . . . I took her to lunch in town and she criticized me—now what do you think about?

KENNETH
[*Sitting on arm of chair.*]
For once my intuition fails me.

LEONIE
About my technique with men. She said it was lousy. Isn't it delicious?

KENNETH
Not more specific than simply lousy?

LEONIE
She said I threw myself at men instead of reversing the process.

END OF SUMMER

KENNETH

But I should think she would have approved of that. She makes such a fetish of being candid!

LEONIE

That's just what I said—exactly. I said I couldn't pretend—that I couldn't descend to—technique. I said that when my feelings were involved I saw no point in not letting the other person see it. I reproached her for deviousness. Strange ideas that child has—strange!

KENNETH

I'm afraid her generation is theory-ridden!
[*Pause.*]

LEONIE

Kenneth?

KENNETH

Yes, Leonie?

LEONIE

It's true of course.

KENNETH

What?

LEONIE

Paula's—criticism. I can't conceal my feelings. Least of all—from you.
[*Slight pause.*]

END OF SUMMER

KENNETH
Why should you?

LEONIE
Oh, Kenneth, I'm so useless! You know how useless I am!

KENNETH
I know only that you are gracious and lovely—and that you have the gift of innocence.

LEONIE
I hate my life. It's been so scattered—emotionally.

KENNETH
Whose isn't?

LEONIE
You are such a comfort. Really it's too much now to expect me to do without you. Kenneth?

KENNETH
Yes . . . Leonie.

LEONIE
Will you be a darling—and marry me?

KENNETH
Leonie?

END OF SUMMER

LEONIE
[*Returning his gaze.*]
Yes, Kenneth.

KENNETH
Have you thought this over?

LEONIE
It's the first time—the very first time—that I've ever been sure.

KENNETH
You are so impulsive, Leonie.

LEONIE
Kenneth, don't you think we'd have a chance—you and I—don't you think?
[*Enter* PAULA, *door back.*]

PAULA
[*Realizes she has interrupted a tête-à-tête.*]
Oh, sorry—!

LEONIE
Paula dear, have you been with Mother?

PAULA
Yes. Granny wants to see you, as a matter of fact.

LEONIE
Oh, I forgot! Is she all right? Cheerful?

PAULA
Oh, very.

LEONIE
I'll be right there. Stay and talk to Kenneth, Paula. He thinks you don't like him. Prove to him it isn't true. Do you think you could be gracious, Paula? Or is that too old-fashioned?

[*Exit* LEONIE *door back. In the following scene* PAULA *determines to get rid of the tantalizing and irritating mixed feelings she has about* KENNETH, *her sense of distrusting, disliking and simultaneously being fascinated by him—she feels he has something up his sleeve; she is playing a game to discover what it is and yet she becomes increasingly conscious that game is not unpleasant to her because of her interest in her victim.*]

PAULA
Leonie's all a-flutter. What is it?

KENNETH
She was just telling me—she envies you your poise.

END OF SUMMER

PAULA

Your intentions are honorable, I hope.

KENNETH

Old hat, Paula.

PAULA

I beg your pardon.

KENNETH

Undergraduate audacity. Scott Fitzgerald. Old hat.

PAULA

We don't like each other much, do we?

KENNETH

That's regrettable.

PAULA

And yet—I'm very curious about you.

KENNETH

What would you like to know?

PAULA

Your motive.

END OF SUMMER

KENNETH

Ah!

PAULA

And yet even if you told me—

KENNETH

You wouldn't believe it?

PAULA

[*Facing him.*]

No. Now why is that? Even when you are perfectly frank your frankness seems to me—a device. Now why is that?

KENNETH

I'll tell you.

PAULA

Why?

KENNETH

Because you yourself are confused, muddled, unsure, contradictory. I am simple and co-ordinated. You resent that. You dislike it. You envy it. You would like such simplicity for yourself. But, as you are unlikely to achieve it, you soothe yourself by distrusting me.

PAULA

You say I'm muddled. Why am I muddled?

END OF SUMMER

KENNETH

You've accepted a set of premises without examining them or thinking about them. You keep them like jewels in a box and dangle them. Then you put them back in the box, confident that they belong to you. But as they don't you feel an occasional twinge of insecurity—

PAULA

Do you mind dropping the parables—?

KENNETH

Not at all—

PAULA

Why am I muddled? For example—

KENNETH

You're a walking contradiction in terms—

PAULA

For example?

KENNETH

For example—for example—your radicalism. Your friends. Your point of view. Borrowed. Unexamined. Insincere.

PAULA

Go on.

KENNETH

You are rich and you are exquisite. Why are you rich and exquisite?

[*Walking back to face her.*]

Because your forbears were not moralistic but ruthless. Had they been moralistic, had they been concerned, as you pretend to be, with the "predatory system"—this awful terminology—you'd be working in a store somewhere wrapping packages or waiting on querulous housewives with bad skins or teaching school. Your own origins won't bear a moralistic investigation. You must know that. Your sociology and economics must teach you that.

PAULA

Suppose I repudiate my origins?

KENNETH

That takes more courage than you have.

PAULA

Don't be so sure.

KENNETH

But why should you? If you had a special talent or were a crusader there might be some sense in it. But you have no special talent and you are not a crusader. Much better to be decorative. Much better for a world

starving for beauty. Instead of repudiating your origins you should exult in them and in that same predatory system that made you possible.
[*Crossing to table behind sofa for cigarette.*]
[*Pause.*]

PAULA
What were your origins?

KENNETH
[*Lighting cigarette.*]
Anonymous.

PAULA
What do you mean?

KENNETH
I was discovered on a doorstep.

PAULA
Really?

KENNETH
Like Moses.

PAULA
Where were you brought up?

KENNETH
In a foundling asylum in New England. The place lacked charm. This sounds like an unpromising begin-

ning but actually it was more stimulating than you might imagine. I remember as a kid of twelve going to the library in Springfield and getting down the *Dictionary of National Biography* and hunting out the bastards. Surprising how many distinguished ones there were and are. I allied myself early with the brilliant and variegated company of the illegitimate.

                        PAULA

You don't know who your parents were?

                       KENNETH

No.

                        PAULA

Did you get yourself through college?

                       KENNETH

And medical school.

                        PAULA

Did you practice medicine?

                       KENNETH

For a bit. I devoted myself—when the victims would let me—to their noses and throats. It was a starveling occupation. But I gave up tonsilectomy for the soul.

END OF SUMMER

The poor have tonsils but only the rich have souls. My instinct was justified—as you see.

PAULA
You've gone pretty far.

KENNETH
Incredible journey!

PAULA
Having come from—from—

KENNETH
The mud—?

PAULA
Well—I should think you'd be more sympathetic to the under-dogs.

KENNETH
No, why should I? The herd bores me. It interests me only as an indication of the distance I've travelled.

PAULA
Will would say that you are a lucky individual who—

KENNETH
Yes, that is what Will would say. It always satisfies the mediocrity to call the exceptional individual lucky.

END OF SUMMER

PAULA

You don't like Will?

KENNETH

I despise him.

PAULA

Why?

KENNETH

I detest these young firebrands whose incandescence will be extinguished by the first job! I detest radicals who lounge about in country-houses.

PAULA

You're unfair to Will.

KENNETH

I have no interest in being fair to him. We were discussing you.

PAULA

You are too persuasive. I don't believe you.

KENNETH

My advice to you is to find out what you want before you commit yourself to young Mr. Dexter.

PAULA

But I have committed myself.

END OF SUMMER

KENNETH

Too bad.

PAULA

For him or for me?

KENNETH

For both of you; but for him particularly.

PAULA

Why?

KENNETH

I see precisely the effect your money will have on him. He will take it and the feeling will grow in him that in having given it you have destroyed what he calls his integrity. He will even come to believe that if not for this quenching of initiative he might have become a flaming leader of the people. At the same time he will be aware that both these comforting alibis are delusions —because he has no integrity to speak of nor any initiative to speak of. Knowing they are lies he will only proclaim them the louder, cling to them the harder. He will hate you as the thief of his character— petty larceny, I must say.

PAULA

[*Jumping up, taking several steps away from him.*]
That's a lie.

KENNETH

Will is an American Puritan. A foreigner—Boris, for example—marries money, feeling that he gives value received. Very often he does. But young Dexter will never feel that—and maybe he'll be right.

PAULA

You hate Will.

KENNETH

You flatter him.

PAULA

How did you get to know so much about people? About what they feel and what they will do?

KENNETH

I began by knowing myself—but not lying to myself.
> [*A silence. He looks at her. He takes in her loveliness. He speaks her name, in a new voice, softly.*]

Paula—

PAULA

[*She looks at him fixedly.*]
What?

KENNETH

Paula—

PAULA
What?

KENNETH
Do you know me any better now? Do you trust me any better now?

PAULA
I don't know.
  [*Enter* WILL.]

KENNETH
Paula, Paula, Paula—
  [PAULA *starts toward door back.*]
Don't go, Paula!

WILL
Oughtn't you to be changing for dinner?
  [PAULA *stops upstage.*]
Hello, Doctor. What's the matter?

KENNETH
May I congratulate him?

WILL
What's he been saying?

KENNETH
Paula told me she is going to marry you.

END OF SUMMER

PAULA
The doctor is a cynic.

KENNETH
We were discussing the European and American points of view toward money marriages—There's a great difference. The European fortune-hunter, once he has landed the bag, has no more twinge of conscience than a big-game hunter when he has made his kill. The American—

WILL
Is that what you think I am, Doctor?

KENNETH
[*To* PAULA *amiably.*]
You see. He resents the mere phrase. But my dear boy, that is no disgrace. We are all fortune-hunters—

PAULA
[*Pointedly.*]
Not all, Kenneth—!

KENNETH
But I see no difference at all between the man who makes a profession of being charming to rich ladies—or any other—specialist. The former is more arduous.

END OF SUMMER

PAULA
Are you defending Will or yourself?

KENNETH
I am generalizing.

[*To* WILL.]

Congratulations! I admit that to scatter congratulations in this way is glib, but we live in a convention of glibness. Good God, we congratulate people when they marry and when they produce children—we skim lightly over these tremendous hazards— Excuse me.

[*Exit* KENNETH.]

WILL
God damn that man!

PAULA
Will!

WILL
I can't stand him—not from the moment I saw him—because he's incapable of disinterestedness himself, he can't imagine it in others. He's the kind of cynical, sneering— He's a marauder. The adventurer with the cure-all. This is just the moment for him. And this is just the place!

PAULA
I've never seen you lose your temper before, Will.

WILL

You know why, don't you?

PAULA

Why?

WILL

Because he's right! While he was talking I felt like hitting him. At the same time a voice inside me said: Can you deny it? When I came in here he was saying your name. He was looking at you—it seems he hasn't quite decided, has he?

PAULA

I'm worried about him and Leonie—

WILL

He's got Leonie hook, line and sinker. That's obvious.

PAULA

She mustn't! Will, she mustn't!

WILL

You can't stop it—you can't do anything for Leonie. Nobody can do anything for anybody. Nobody should try.

PAULA

Will—you mustn't go back to New York. You must stay and help me.

WILL
Sorry. Nothing doing.

PAULA
Will!

WILL
I have a feeling you'll rather enjoy saving Leonie from the doctor.

PAULA
Will! That's not fair, Will!

WILL
It may not be fair but it is obvious. Also, it is obvious that the doctor won't mind being saved.

PAULA
It's lucky for both of us that one of us has some self-control.

WILL
No, I won't stay here. I hate the place, I hate Dr. Rice, I hate myself for being here!

PAULA
Don't let me down, Will—I need you terribly just now—

END OF SUMMER

WILL

[*At white heat.*]

I haven't quite the technique of fortune hunting yet—in the European manner. Which of the two is he after—you or Leonie? Will he flip a coin?

PAULA

I hate you! I hate you!

WILL

Well, we know where we are at any rate.

PAULA

Yes. We do!

[LEONIE *comes running in. She wears an exquisite summer evening frock. She is breathless with happiness.*]

LEONIE

Paula! Why aren't you dressed? I want you to wear something especially lovely tonight! Do you like this? It's new. I haven't worn it before.

[*She twirls for them.*]

I've a surprise for you, Will. You'll know what it is in a minute. I was thinking of you and it popped into my mind. You know, Will, I'm very, very fond of you. And I think you are equally fond of me. I can't help liking people who like me. I suppose you think I'm horribly vain. But then, everybody's vain about something.

    [BUTLER *comes in with cocktails and sandwiches, to table right of fireplace.*]

If they're not, they're vain about their lack of vanity. I believe that's a mot! Pretty good for a brainless— Here, Will, have a cocktail—

    [WILL *takes cockatil.*]

Paula—what's your pet vanity? She thinks mine's my looks but it's not. If I had my way I shouldn't look at all the way I look.

    [*Enter* DR. DEXTER, *door back. He wears a sea-green baggy dinner-suit; he looks as "hicky" and uncertain as ever.*]

DEXTER
Good evening, Mrs. Frothingham.

LEONIE
Dr. Dexter—how good of you to come. Delighted to see you.

DEXTER
Good evening. Hello, Will.

WILL
Dad!

END OF SUMMER

DEXTER
Mrs. Frothingham invited me. Didn't you know?

LEONIE
[*Takes* DEXTER's *arm and goes to* WILL.]
You told me you had to leave tomorrow to visit your father in Brunswick so I just called him up in Brunswick—

DEXTER
She sent the car all the way for me. Nice car. Great springs.

LEONIE
[*To* WILL.]
Now you won't have to leave tomorrow. You can both spend the week-end here.

WILL
[*Walking away a little right.*]
Awfully nice of you, Leonie.

LEONIE
[*Following him.*]
[DEXTER *sits on sofa.*]
You see, Will, I leave the big issues to the professional altruists. I just do what I can toward making those around me happy. And that's *my* vanity!
[*Enter* DENNIS, *door back.*]

END OF SUMMER

DENNIS

Well! Well! Fancy that now, Hedda!

LEONIE

Oh, hello, Dennis, just in time for a cocktail.
[LEONIE *leads him over to sofa.* WILL *is isolated down right center.*]

DENNIS

[*To* DEXTER.]
How are you?

DEXTER

[*Not friendly.*]
I'm all right.

DENNIS

Complicated week-end! You and the Healer! Faraday and Cagliostro. That'll be something.

LEONIE

[*Takes Dennis's arm.*]
Everybody tells me to like you, Dennis. I'm in such a mood that I'm going to make the effort.

DENNIS

I've been waiting for this. I'm thrilled!

END OF SUMMER

LEONIE
[*Strolling with him across stage front.*]
Something tells me you could be very charming if you wanted to. Tell me, Dennis, have you ever tried being lovable and sweet?

DENNIS
For you, Mrs. Frothingham, I would willingly revive the age of chivalry!

LEONIE
But there's no need of that. I just want you to be nice. Here, have a cocktail. Give you courage.

DENNIS
Just watch me from now on, Mrs. Frothingham.

LEONIE
I will. Passionately.
[*Hands him cocktail.*]
I'll be doing nothing else.
[BUTLER *crosses back of sofa, offers* DEXTER *and* PAULA *cocktails.* DR. RICE *comes in.*]

DENNIS
[*Stage sigh.*]
Ah-h-h! The doctor! Just in time to look at my tongue, Doctor.

END OF SUMMER

KENNETH

That won't be necessary, young man. I can tell—It's excessive.

LEONIE

[*Crossing to* KENNETH.]
Kenneth—you remember Will's father—Dr. Dexter.

KENNETH

How do you do?

[*They shake hands. A second* BUTLER *has come in and he and* ROBERT *are passing cocktails and hors d'œuvres.* LEONIE *keeps circulating among her guests.* KENNETH *and* DEXTER *are in the center—*DENNIS, *obeying a malicious impulse, presides over them. Announces a theme on which he eggs them on to utter variations.*]

DENNIS

A significant moment, ladies and gentlemen—the magician of Science meets the magician of Sex—The floating libido bumps the absolute! What happens?

DEXTER

[*Cupping his hand to his ear.*]
What?

[WILL *crosses to door and looks out moodily.*]

DENNIS

The absolute hasn't got a chance. Isn't that right, Dr. Rice?

KENNETH

I shouldn't venture to contradict a young intellectual. Especially a very young intellectual.

LEONIE

[*Crosses front of* KENNETH, *to* DENNIS.]

There, you see, I'm afraid, after all, I'll have to give you up, Dennis. You can't be lovable. You can't be sweet.

DENNIS

But I didn't promise to be winsome to everybody, only to you.

LEONIE

You really must treat him, Kenneth. He has no censor at all.

DENNIS

My censor is the Catholic tradition. We Catholics anticipated both Marx and Freud by a little matter of nineteen centuries. Spiritually, we have a Communion in the Holy Ghost—Communion. As for Dr. Rice, he offers confession without absolution. He is inadequate.

[LEONIE *returns with tray of canapes.*]

LEONIE

It seems such bad taste to discuss religion at cocktail time. Try a stuffed olive.

END OF SUMMER

DEXTER

By the time you got your beautiful new world, true science will have perished.

LEONIE

Aren't you too pessimistic, Dr. Dexter? Too much science has made you gloomy. Kenneth, the depression hasn't stopped your work, has it? Depression or no depression—

[WILL *springs up.*]

WILL

[*Tensely.*]
That's right, Leonie.
[*Everyone faces* WILL.]
Depression or no depression—war or peace—revolution or reaction—Kenneth will reign supreme!
[KENNETH *stares at him.* WILL *confronts him.*]

LEONIE

Will!

WILL

Yes, Leonie. His is the power and the glory!

LEONIE

Dennis, this is your influence—

END OF SUMMER

WILL

I admire you unreservedly, Doctor. Of your kind you are the best. You are the essence.

KENNETH

You embarrass me.

WILL

Some men are born ahead of their time, some behind, but you are made pat for the instant. Now is the time for you—when people are unemployed and distrust their own capacities—when people suffer and may be tempted—when integrity yields to despair—now is the moment for you!

KENNETH

[*Strolling closer to him so they are face to face.*]
When, may I ask, is the moment for you—when if ever?

WILL

After your victory. When you are stuffed and inert with everything you want, then will be the time for me.
[*He goes out.*]

PAULA

[*Running after* WILL.]
Will . . . Will . . . Will . . .
[*She follows him out.*]

LEONIE

[*Devastated by this strange behavior.*]
What is it? I don't like it when people stand in the middle of the floor and make speeches. What's the matter with him? Dennis, do you know?

DENNIS

[*With a look at* KENNETH.]
I can guess.

LEONIE

Has he quarreled with Paula? Paula is so inept. She doesn't know how to . . . At the same time, if he had a grievance, why couldn't he have kept it until after dinner?

[*Enter* ROBERT.]

ROBERT

Dinner is served.

[*Exit* ROBERT.]

LEONIE

Well, we'll do what we can. Sam is dining with Mother in her room, Boris has a headache. Dennis, you and Dr. Dexter—

DENNIS

You've picked me, Dr. Dexter. I congratulate you.

DEXTER

Thank God, I can't hear a word you say.
[*Exit* DEXTER, *door back.*]

DENNIS

[*Sadistically.*]
Oh, yes, he can. And we'll fight it out on these lines if it takes all dinner.
[*He follows* DEXTER *out.*]

LEONIE

What extraordinary behavior! What do you suppose, Kenneth—shall I go after them?

KENNETH

I wouldn't. It's their problem. Give them time.

LEONIE

[*Reassured.*]
You are so wise, Kenneth. How did I ever get on without you? I have that secure feeling that you are going to be my last indiscretion. When I think how neatly I've captured you—I feel quite proud. I guess my technique isn't so lousy after all.
[*She takes his arm and swings along beside him as they waltz in to dinner.*]

Curtain

ACT THREE

ACT THREE

Scene: *The same.*

Time: Late that fall. The trees have turned. The sumach have put out the brilliant red flowers of autumn.

At Rise: Will *and* Dennis *have just arrived, and are standing at fireplace, back.* Leonie *comes in to greet them.* Sam *strolls in with her.*

LEONIE
I'm so glad to see you!
[*She shakes hands with each of them warmly.*]
Will! How are you?
[*To* Dennis.]
It's so good of you to come.

SAM
[*Shaking hands with* Will.]
Very glad to see you.

WILL
Thanks.
[Sam *shakes hands with* Dennis.]

LEONIE

Sam drove over for a few hours from Blue Hill to talk business to me. He hasn't had much luck so far. It's simply wonderful having you boys here—it's like old times. I didn't tell Paula.

[*To* SAM.]

I did all this on my own. It's a surprise for Paula.

DENNIS

She'll be overcome when she sees me. Maybe you should prepare her.

WILL

Where is Paula?

LEONIE

Isn't it provoking! She and Kenneth went for a walk. They should have been back long before this.

[*Turning back to them.*]

Paula hasn't been at all herself, Will. I thought you would cheer her up.

DENNIS

I will be glad to do what I can, of course. Several very stubborn cases have yielded to my charm.

LEONIE

I'm sure! Do sit down.

[*She sits.*]

END OF SUMMER

DENNIS

[*Taking out his pipe.*]
Do you mind?
[W̱ɪʟʟ *sits.*]

LEONIE

Oh, please—I can't tell you how I appreciate your coming—

DENNIS

[*The harassed business man.*]
Well, as a matter of fact, Leonie, it wasn't easy to get away from the office—

LEONIE

Are you in an office?

DENNIS

Sometimes as many as fifteen in a day.
[Lᴇᴏɴɪᴇ *laughs.*]
But when I got your appealing letter—*and* the return tickets—I'm chivalrous at heart, you know, Leonie—

LEONIE

I know you are!

SAM

How's town?

END OF SUMMER

WILL

Very hot.

SAM

I'm just on my way down. Stopped by to go over several things with Leonie—

LEONIE

Poor Sam's been having an awful time with me. He keeps putting things in escrow. Where is escrow?

DENNIS

It's where squirrels put nuts in the winter-time.

LEONIE

I see! Dennis is much more lucid than you, Sam.

DENNIS

I have a knack for making the abstruse translucent. Especially in economics. Now, would you like to know why England went off gold?

LEONIE

No, I wouldn't.

DENNIS

I shall yield to your subconscious demand and tell you.

END OF SUMMER

LEONIE

[*To others.*]
Help!

DENNIS

I see that there is no audience for my peculiar gift.

LEONIE

You know, Will, I've thought perhaps you were angry with us.

WILL

Why?

LEONIE

You haven't been here for so long.
[*To* SAM.]
Since Granny died—none of them have been here. Did Paula write you about Granny's funeral?

WILL

No. She didn't.

LEONIE

Of course I hate funerals—I can't bear them—but this was so—natural. Mother wanted to live till the fall and she did. It was a dreaming blue sky and there was that poignant haze over the hills and over the bay, and the smell of burning wood from somewhere. Burning wood never smells at any other time the way it does in Indian summer. And the colors that day! Did you ever, Sam, see such a day?

SAM

It was beautiful.

LEONIE

They say the colors of autumn are the colors of death, but I don't believe that. They were in such strength that day. I cried—but not on account of Mother—that kind of day always makes me cry a little bit anyway. You couldn't cry over consigning anyone you loved to an earth like that—on a day like that. I put some blazing leaves over her, but when I passed there the other day, they were withered and brown—

SAM

[*Chiding her.*]
Now Leonie—

LEONIE

Sam thinks I shouldn't talk about Mother. But I don't see why. She doesn't depress me. I think of her with joy. She had a wonderful life.

SAM

She was a wonderful woman.

LEONIE

[*To* WILL.]

Imagine, Will—when Sam was here last time—you were here that week-end—she *knew*. She asked Sam to be executor of her will.

SAM

[*Very annoyed at her for bringing this up.*]
Leonie—

LEONIE

Why didn't you tell me, Sam, then?

SAM

Seemed no point.

LEONIE

She didn't want me to know, did she?

SAM

No. She didn't want to distress you.
[*A moment's pause.*]

LEONIE

What can be keeping Paula?
[*She glances out of the window.*]
Sam, do you want to talk business to me some more?

SAM
I'd like to talk to Will a minute.

LEONIE
Oh—yes. Well, Dennis, wouldn't you like me to show you to your room?

[*She rises, goes to door into hallway.* DENNIS *follows.*]

DENNIS
Thanks. I've got to answer a chain letter.

LEONIE
I've given you a room you've never had. The tower room.

DENNIS
Is it ivory? I won't be comfortable if it isn't ivory.

LEONIE
Well just this once you're going to be uncomfortable —and like it!

[*She goes out.*]

DENNIS
[*Tragically.*]

And for this I gave up a superb view of the gas-house on 149th Street.

[*He goes out.*]

SAM

[*Rises and goes up toward fireplace.*]
Will—

WILL

Yes, Mr. Frothingham.

SAM

Oh—call me Sam.

WILL

All right.

SAM

I'll have to be pushing off in an hour or so. I rather wanted to talk to you.

WILL

Yes—

SAM

[*Wipes his forehead.*]
Gosh, Leonie's a difficult woman to talk business to. [*Sits.*]

WILL

I can imagine that. She's not interested in business.

SAM

She—is—not!!!

END OF SUMMER

WILL

What do you want to speak to me about?

SAM

Paula.

WILL

What about Paula?

SAM

As I'm her father—I hope you won't think me—

WILL

Of course not—

SAM

It's not altogether easy—

WILL

Do you want me to help you?

SAM

Yes. I wish you would!

WILL

You're worried about Paula and me, aren't you? So was her grandmother. You think me irresponsible. Less responsible for example—[*As if making a random comparison*] than Dr. Rice?

END OF SUMMER

SAM

Well, as a matter of fact, I've rather gotten to know Dr. Rice, and in many respects, he's a pretty sound feller.

[*Rising and going to stand above* WILL.]

Hang it all, Will, I like you, and I don't like to preach to you, you know.

WILL

Go on.

SAM

Well, there are—from my point of view at least—a lot of nonsensical ideas knocking about. I'd like to point out just one thing to you. Your radicalism and all that— Well, the point is this—if you marry Paula—and I hope you do, because I like you—and, what is more important, Paula likes you—you'll have responsibilities. Paula will be rich. Very rich. Money means responsibility. Now, I shouldn't, for example, like you to start radical magazines with it. I shouldn't like you to let the money drift through your fingers in all sorts of aimless, millennial directions that won't get anywhere.

WILL

Who told you that was my intention?

SAM

A little bird.

END OF SUMMER

WILL
With a black moustache?

SAM
Does that matter?

WILL
No.

SAM
[*Putting hand on* WILL's *shoulder.*]
As a matter of fact, I'm not worried about you at all. Money, I expect, will do to you what getting power does to radical opposition, once it gets office—

WILL
Emasculate me, you mean?

SAM
Well, hardly. Mature you. Once you're rich yourself, I have no doubt you'll be—

WILL
Sound.

SAM
Yes. Sound. But your friends—this McCarthy boy—

END OF SUMMER

WILL

Well, I can easily cut Dennis—all my poor and unsound friends—

SAM

[*Quietly.*]
I'm sorry you're taking this tone with me, Will. I'm the last person in the world to ask you to drop anybody. I'd be ashamed of you if you did. Only—

WILL

Only?

SAM

I must tell you that I am in position—by virtue of the will left by Mrs. Wyler—to keep Paula's money from being used for any purpose that might be construed as—subversive.

WILL

From whose point of view?

SAM

[*Quietly.*]
From mine.

WILL

I see.

SAM

Possibly you may not believe this—but I trust you, Will. Mrs. Wyler trusted you.

END OF SUMMER

WILL

You needn't worry. Paula seems to have other interests apparently.

SAM

What do you mean?

WILL

Sounder interests—
[DENNIS *enters, through door back.*]

DENNIS

The tower room lets in light on four sides, but nothing to look at. Just the sea and the landscape.

SAM

What did you do with Leonie?

DENNIS

She's gone to her mother's room to potter around.

SAM

Maybe I can get her attention while she's pottering. Excuse me.
[SAM *goes out.*]

DENNIS

Poor Leonie—she's the last of the lovely ladies. The inheritance taxes'll get 'em soon. You know we were

END OF SUMMER

by way of getting our magazine from Leonie when Dr. Rice spiked our guns. So I'm leaving. My time is too valuable. But the Healer won't last forever, and when he goes, I shall return. Take heart, my good man. I know you feel a little tender about doing this, but remember, my lad, it's the Cause that counts. Remember what Shaw says: "There is no money but the devil's money. It is all tainted and it might as well be used in the service of God."

> [*A moment—*WILL *is obviously thinking of something else.*]

What's the matter?

WILL

Nothing.

DENNIS

> [*Bringing down chair to sit left of* WILL *he imitates* RICE's *manner.*]

Now you must speak, young man—how can I sublimate your subconscious troubles, if you won't speak? Are you unhappy about Paula, my lad?

> [*No answer.*]

Tell me what's happened between you—relieve your soul, and, as a reward, I may make you co-editor of our magazine.

> [*No response. He rises and walks to opposite side of table.*]

No? Assistant editor you remain. I may even fire you. Yes, I think I will fire you.
   [Crossing in front of WILL *to fireplace.]*
Dexter—you're through. Go upstairs and get your check.
   [Rubs his hands together in glee.]
God, it gives me a sense of power to fire a man—especially an old friend!
   *[*PAULA *and* KENNETH *come in door right from the garden.]*

PAULA

[Amazed to see them.]
Will! But how—! Dennis!

WILL

[Rather coolly.]
Hello, Paula.

DENNIS

We came to surprise you. Now that we have surprised you, we can go home.

WILL

Leonie asked me to come.

PAULA

Oh. Well, it's very nice to see you.

END OF SUMMER

WILL
Thanks.

PAULA
When I wired you to come a few weeks ago, you were too busy. It takes Leonie, doesn't it?

DENNIS
You should have tried me, Paula. Hello, Dr. Rice. How's business? Any suppressions today?

KENNETH
[*Significantly.*]
Apparently not.

DENNIS
Well, come on up to my room, Doctor, and we'll play Twenty Questions.
[*He goes out.*]

WILL
Hello, Dr. Rice.

KENNETH
How are you?

PAULA
Will—I'm awfully glad to see you. I was just going to write you to thank you for the sweet letter you sent me after Granny died.

END OF SUMMER

KENNETH

I'm afraid it's my fault, Dexter. I do my best to keep Paula so busy that she finds no time to write letters.

WILL

I was sure I could count on you, Doctor.
[WILL *goes out.*]

PAULA

You enjoy hurting Will, don't you?

KENNETH

When there is an obstacle in my path, I do my best to remove it.

PAULA

What makes you think it is only Will that stands between us— That if left to myself I—

KENNETH

Because it is true. Were it not for the squids of idealistic drivel spouted around you by Will and his friends, there would be no issue at all between us. I resent even an imputed rivalry with someone I despise.

PAULA

Rivalry?

END OF SUMMER

KENNETH

Paula— There's no reason any longer why I shouldn't tell you the truth.

PAULA

What is it, Kenneth?

KENNETH

[*After a moment—slowly.*]

Do you know what I feel like? I feel like a man on a great height, irresistibly tempted to jump over. Do you want the truth really?

[*She says nothing. Somehow his words, his voice, his attitude make her feel that really now he may reveal something which before he wouldn't have revealed. He is in a trance-like state almost; she feels it; she is rather horribly fascinated —somehow, though she distrusts him utterly, some instinct tells her that, at this moment actually he is tempted by a force, disruptive to himself, to tell her the truth.*]

Don't you know it? Don't you feel it?

[*Pause.*]

Haven't you known it? Haven't you felt it?

[*A moment's pause.*]

I love you.

END OF SUMMER

PAULA

What?

KENNETH

I love you.

[*A pause. She is too stupefied to speak. She too is under a spell. She is fascinated by him—by the enormity of this. She rises, walks away from him to stand by sofa.*]

PAULA

I suppose I should be afraid of you. I'm not afraid of you.

KENNETH

I am afraid of you. You tempt me to venture the impossible. That is impractical. And I have always been eminently practical.

PAULA

I'm sure you have.

[*She feels herself talking automatically, as if out of a hypnotic state—at the same time some vanity and shrewdness keeps pounding inside her: "See how far he will go—see how far he will go!"*]

KENNETH

I have lived by a plan. The plan has matured. But I have yearned for a face that would give me joy, for the voice that would soothe me. It is your face. It is your voice.

[PAULA *is fighting not to scream; at the same time she is caught in a nightmarish fascination.*]

PAULA

[*Very faintly.*]
Don't you love Mother?

KENNETH

No.

[*A moment's pause.*]
You are the youth I have never had, the security I have never had—you are the home I have hungered for.

[*Moves toward her—stands over her and a little back.*]

That I am standing near you now, that I have achieved a share in your life, that you are listening to me, that you are thinking of me and of what I am, to the exclusion of everything else in the whirling universe—this is a miracle so devastating, that it makes any future possible—Paula—

PAULA

What?

KENNETH

Paula!

END OF SUMMER

PAULA

What *is* it!

KENNETH

[*Bending over her.*]
Paula . . .
  [*It is as if he got a sexual joy from saying her name.*]
I love your name. I love to say your name.

PAULA

I *am* afraid of you. I'm sorry for you.

KENNETH

Do you think me insane?

PAULA

Yes.

KENNETH

Because I am ambitious, because I am forthright, because I deal scientifically with the human stuff around me—you think me insane. Because I am ruthless and romantic, you think me insane. This boy you think you love—who spends his time sniveling about a system he is not strong enough to dominate—is he sane?

PAULA

I don't expect you to—

END OF SUMMER

KENNETH

When I hear the chatter of your friends, it makes me sick. While they and their kind prate of co-operative commonwealths, the strong man takes power, and rides over their backs—which is all their backs are fit for. Never has the opportunity for the individual career been so exalted, so infinite in its scope, so horizonal. House-painters and minor journalists become dictators of great nations.

[*With puckish humor—leaning on arm of her chair.*]

Imagine what a really clever man could do! See what he has done!

[*He smiles, makes a gesture of modest self-assertion, indicating the room as part of his conquest. She laughs, rather choked and embarrassed. He goes on.*]

And this I have done alone. From an impossible distance—I have come to you, so that when I speak, you can hear. What might we not do together, Paula—you and I—

[*To her surprise,* PAULA *finds herself arguing an inconceivable point. She loathes the strange fascination she feels in this man, and yet is aware that it might turn to her advantage.*]

END OF SUMMER

PAULA

We don't want the same things.

KENNETH

You want what everyone wants who has vitality and imagination—new forms of power—new domains of knowledge—the ultimate sensations.

PAULA

You *are* romantic, aren't you?

KENNETH

Endlessly. And endlessly—realistic.
[*Staring at her.*]
What are you thinking?

PAULA

[*Shrewd against him—against herself.*]
I keep thinking—what you want now—what you're after now?

KENNETH

[*Moving toward her.*]
You don't believe then—that I love you?

PAULA

[*Leaning back in chair—not looking at him.*]
You are a very strange man.

END OF SUMMER

KENNETH

I am simple really. I want everything. That's all!

PAULA

And you don't care how you get it.

KENNETH

Don't be moralistic, Paula—I beg you. I am directly in the tradition of your own marauding ancestors. They pass now for pioneers—actually they fell on the true pioneers, and wrested what they had found away from them, by sheer brutal strength. I am doing the same thing—but more adroitly.

PAULA

Why are you so honest with me?

KENNETH

[*With his most charming smile.*]

Perhaps because I feel that, in your heart, you too are an adventurer.

[*A pause. During these half-spell-bound instants a thought has been forming slowly in* PAULA'S *mind that crystallizes now. This man is the enemy. This man is infinitely cunning, infinitely resourceful. Perhaps—just the possibility—he really feels this passion for her. If so, why not use this weakness in an antagonist so ruthless? She will try.*]

PAULA

I shouldn't listen to you—
  [*A moment. He senses her cunning. He looks at her.*]

KENNETH

You don't trust me?

PAULA

Have I reason to trust you?

KENNETH

What reason would you like? What proof would you like?

PAULA

Aren't you going to marry Mother?

KENNETH

Only as an alternative.

PAULA

Will you—tell her so? Will you give up the alternative?

KENNETH

And if I do?

PAULA
What shall I promise you?

KENNETH
Yourself.

PAULA
[*Looks at him—speaks.*]
And if I do?

KENNETH
Then . . .

PAULA
[*Taking fire.*]
You say you love me! If you feel it—really feel it—You haven't been very adventurous for all your talk! Taking in Mother and Sam! Give up those conquests. Tell her! Tell Mother! Then perhaps I will believe you.

KENNETH
And then?

PAULA
Take your chances!

KENNETH
[*Quietly.*]
Very well.

PAULA
You will?

END OF SUMMER

KENNETH

I will.

PAULA

You'll tell Mother—you love me?

KENNETH

Yes.

PAULA

[*Going to the foot of the stairs, calls:*]
Mother! Mother!

LEONIE

[*Offstage.*]
Yes, Paula. I'm coming right down! I've the most marvelous surprise for you! Wait and see!
   [PAULA *walks to end of sofa—looking at* KENNETH. LEONIE *comes in. She is wearing an exquisite old-fashioned silk wedding-dress which billows around her in an immense shimmering circle. She is a vision of enchantment.*]

LEONIE

[*In a great flurry of excitement.*]
Children, look what I found! It's Mother's. It's the dress she was married in. I was poking around in Granny's room while Sam was talking to me about bonds, and I came upon it. Do you like it, Kenneth?

END OF SUMMER

Isn't it adorable? Have you ever . . . What's the matter? Don't you like it?

PAULA

It's very pretty.

LEONIE

[*Overwhelmed by the inadequacy of this word.*]
Pretty! Pretty!

[*She hopes for more from* KENNETH.]
Kenneth . . . ?

KENNETH

It's exquisite.

LEONIE

Isn't it?

[*She whirls around in the dress.*]
Isn't it? Yes. Exquisite. Can you imagine the scene? Can you imagine Granny walking down the aisle—and all the august spectators in mutton-chop whiskers and Prince Alberts? We've lost something these days—a good deal—oh, I don't miss the mutton-chops—but in ceremony, I mean—in punctilio and grace. . . .

PAULA

[*Cutting ruthlessly through the nostalgia.*]
Mother!

LEONIE

What is it, Paula?

END OF SUMMER

PAULA
Kenneth has something to tell you.

LEONIE
Kenneth?

PAULA
Yes. He has something to tell you.

LEONIE
Have you, Kenneth?

KENNETH
Yes.

LEONIE
What is it?

KENNETH
[*Quietly.*]
I love Paula. I want to marry Paula.
[*A pause. Granny's wedding-dress droops.*]

LEONIE
Do you mean that, Kenneth?

KENNETH
Yes.

LEONIE
[*Piteously.*]
This isn't very nice of you, Paula.

PAULA
I had nothing to do with it. I loathe Kenneth. But I wanted you to know him. Now you see him, Mother, your precious Lothario—there he is! Look at him!

LEONIE
These clothes are picturesque, but I think our modern ones are more comfortable. I think—I feel quite faint—isn't it ridiculous?
[*She sways.*]
PAULA
I'm sorry, Mother. I had to. But I love you. I really do.
LEONIE
[*Very faint.*]
Thank you, Paula.

PAULA
You'd better go up and lie down. I'll come to you in a moment.
LEONIE
Yes. I think I'd better. Yes.
[*She begins to sob; she goes out, hiding her face in the lace folds of her dress.* PAULA, *having gone with her to the door, rings bell for* ROBERT, *turns to* KENNETH.]

END OF SUMMER

PAULA

I suppose you're going to tell me this isn't cricket. Well, don't, because it will only make me laugh. To live up to a code with people like you is only to be weak and absurd.

KENNETH

[*His voice is low and even but tense with hate.*]
You, Miss Frothingham, are my *last* miscalculation. I might even say my first. Fortunately, not irreparable!
[ROBERT *enters.*]

PAULA

Robert.

ROBERT

Yes, Miss Frothingham.

PAULA

[*Still staring fixedly at* KENNETH.]
Dr. Rice is leaving. Will you see that his bags are packed, please?

ROBERT

Yes, Miss.
[*He goes out.*]

KENNETH

Forgive me—for having over-estimated you.
[*He goes out door right.* PAULA *comes slowly*

down and sits on sofa. She gets a reaction herself now from all she has been through; this game hasn't been natural to her; she is trembling physically; she is on the verge of tears. WILL *comes in.*]

PAULA

Will—Will darling—
[*She clings to* WILL.]

WILL

[*Worried.*]
Paula!

PAULA

Put your arms around me, Will—hold me close—
[WILL *obeys.*]

WILL

What's happened?

PAULA

I've tricked him. I made him say in front of Mother that he loved me, that he wanted to marry me. Poor Leonie! But it had to be done! And do you know, Will—at the end I felt—gosh, one has so many selves, Will. I must tell you—for the—well, for the completeness of the record—

END OF SUMMER

WILL

[*Curious.*]
What?

PAULA

At the end I felt I had to do it—not only to save Leonie—but to save myself. Can you understand that? I felt horribly drawn to him, and by the sordid thing I was doing— But it's over. Thank God it's over. Will, darling, these six weeks have been hell without you. When I got your letter about Granny, I sat down and cried. I wanted to go right to New York to be with you. And yet I couldn't. How could I? But now, Will—I don't want to wait for you any longer. I've done what I can. It's cost me almost— Will—I need you terribly—

WILL

And I you, Paula. But listen, darling—I've decided during the weeks I've been away from you— I can't marry you now— I can't face what I'd become—

PAULA

But Will, I—
[*Springing up.*]
But Will, I'll give up the money. I'll live with you anywhere.

WILL

I know that, Paula. But I mustn't. You mustn't let me. I've thought it all out. You say you'd live with me anywhere. But what would happen? Supposing I didn't get a job? Would we starve? We'd take fifty dollars a week from your grandmother's estate. It would be foolish not to. Taking fifty, why not seventy-five? Why not two hundred? I can't let myself in for it, Paula.

[*A long pause.*]

Paula, darling—do you hate me?

PAULA

No.

WILL

Supposing you weren't rich? Is it a world in which, but for this, I'd have to sink? If it is, I'm going to damn well do what I can to change it. I don't have to scrabble for the inheritance of dead men. That's for Kenneth—one robber baron—after the lapse of several generations—succeeding another. I don't want this damn fortune to give me an unfair advantage over people as good as I am who haven't got it.

[*Torn with pity for her.*]

Paula—my dearest—what can I do?

END OF SUMMER

PAULA

I see that you can't do anything. I quite see. Still—

WILL

I love you, Paula, and I'll be longing for you terribly, but I can't marry you—not till there's somebody for you to marry. When I've struck my stride, I won't care about Sam, or the money, or anything, because I'll be on my own. If you feel the way I do, you'll wait.

PAULA

[*Very still voice.*]
Of course, Will. I'll wait.

WILL

[*Overcome with gratitude and emotion—seizes her in his arms passionately.*]
Darling—darling—
[LEONIE *comes in.* WILL, *overcome with emotion, goes out.*]

LEONIE

It's easy to say "lie down." But what happens then? Thoughts assail you. Thoughts . . .

PAULA

Mother . . .

END OF SUMMER

LEONIE
Kenneth's going. He's leaving. I suppose you're happy. It's the end—the end of summer.

PAULA
[*Herself shaken with emotion.*]
Mother—
[*She wants to talk to* LEONIE, *to tell her what has happened, but* LEONIE *is lost in her own maze.*]

LEONIE
It's cold here. I hate this place. I'm going to sell it.
[*She sits, in chair, right of fireplace.*]
I've always wanted things around me to be gay and warm and happy. I've done my best. I must be wrong. Why do I find myself this way? With nothing. With nothing.

PAULA
[*Running to her mother and throwing herself on her knees beside her.*]
Mother—Mother darling—

LEONIE
[*Not responding, reflectively.*]
I suppose the thing about me that is wrong is that love is really all I care about.

[*A moment's pause.*]
I suppose I should have been interested in other things. Good works. Do they sustain you? But I couldn't somehow. I think when you're not in love—you're dead. Yes, that must be why I'm . . .
    [*Her voice trails off rather.* PAULA *drops her head in her mother's lap and begins to cry.*]

LEONIE

[*Surprised.*]
Paula—what is it? What's the matter? Are you sorry? It's all right, child.

PAULA

[*Through her tears.*]
It's Will—

LEONIE

Will?

PAULA

He's going away.

LEONIE

Why don't you go with him?

PAULA

He doesn't want me.

LEONIE
That's not true. It must be something else.

PAULA
The money.

LEONIE
Oh, the money. Yes, the money. The money won't do anything for you. It'll work against you. It's worked against me. It gives you the illusion of escape —but always you have to come back to yourself. At the end of every journey—you find yourself.

PAULA
What shall I do, Mother?

LEONIE
You and Will want the same things. In the end you will find them. But don't let him find them with someone else. Follow him. Be near him. When he is depressed and discouraged, let it be your hand that he touches, your face that he sees.

PAULA
[*Breathless.*]
Mother—you're right—he told me last summer—"you must have a shoulder to lean on"—

END OF SUMMER

LEONIE

Let it be your shoulder, Paula; follow him. Be near him.

PAULA

Thank you, Mother.

LEONIE

[*Ruefully.*]
I am telling you what *I* should do. It must be bad advice.

PAULA

[*Gratefully.*]
Darling!
[DENNIS *and* WILL *come in.*]

DENNIS

Here you are! We're off to the boat! Thirty minutes! Why don't you and Paula come too? What do you say, Leonie?

LEONIE

You know, all these years I've been coming up here, and I've never been on the Bar Harbor boat.

DENNIS

It may be said, Mrs. Frothingham, if you have never been on the Bar Harbor boat, that you have not lived!

END OF SUMMER

LEONIE
Really! I'd always heard it was poky.

DENNIS
Poky! The *Normandie* of the Kennebec poky! Mrs. Frothingham!

LEONIE
It's fun, is it? But doesn't it get into New York at some impossible hour?

DENNIS
At seven A.M.

LEONIE
Seven!
[*She shudders.*]

DENNIS
[*The brisk executive.*]
Seven! Yes, sir! At my desk at nine! All refreshed and co-ordinated and ready to attack my South American correspondence.

LEONIE
I must learn not to believe him, mustn't I?

DENNIS
I am my own master, Leonie. All day for nine mortal hours I grind out escape fiction for the pulp maga-

zines. But one day I shall become famous and emerge into the slicks and then I doubt very much whether I shall come here.

LEONIE

I shall miss you.

DENNIS

Then I'll come.

LEONIE

I hate to have you go, Dennis. You cheer me up. Why don't you stay?

DENNIS

Impossible, Leonie. I must go to New York to launch the magazine. But for the moment, good-bye, Leonie. As a reward for your hospitality I shall send you the original copy of one of my stories. Would you like to escape from something?

LEONIE

[*Smiling wanly.*]
I would indeed!

DENNIS

Think no more about it. You're as good as free. The story is yours, typed personally on my Underwood.

Those misplaced keys—those inaccuracies—how they will bemuse posterity!

[*He goes out.*]

WILL

[*Awkwardly.*]
Good-bye, Leonie.

LEONIE

Good-bye, Will.

[*He goes out without looking at* PAULA. *In pantomime,* LEONIE *urges* PAULA *to go after him.* PAULA *kisses her quickly and runs out after* WILL. *Left alone,* LEONIE *walks to the chair in which her mother sat so often—she looks through the glowing autumn at the darkening sea.* KENNETH *comes in. There is a pause.*]

KENNETH

Leonie—

LEONIE

Yes, Kenneth.

KENNETH

I don't expect you to understand this. I shall not try to make you understand it.

END OF SUMMER

LEONIE

Perhaps I'd better not.

KENNETH

Really I am amused at myself—highly entertained. That I should have almost had to practice on myself what hitherto I have reserved for my patients—that I who have made such a fetish of discipline and restraint so nearly succumbed to an inconsistency. I must revise my notion of myself.

LEONIE

And I too.

KENNETH

Why? Why you?

LEONIE

I seem to be a survival—Paula's directness—and your calculations—they are beyond me.

KENNETH

Nevertheless, it's curious how you and Paula are alike—no wonder that, for a moment at least, you seemed to me—interchangeable.

LEONIE

Did you know it from the beginning—that it was Paula?

END OF SUMMER

KENNETH

I was attracted by her resemblance to you—for exercising this attraction I hated her. She felt it too—from the beginning and she must have hated me from the beginning. Between us there grew up this strange, unnatural antagonism—

LEONIE

What?

KENNETH

This fused emotion of love and hate. It had to be brought out into the open. It's a familiar psychosis—the unconscious desire of the daughter to triumph over the mother.

LEONIE

But I don't understand—

KENNETH

There is so much in these intricate relationships that the layman can't understand—

LEONIE

You mean that you—felt nothing for Paula?

KENNETH

No, I don't mean that at all. But I saw that what I felt for her was some twisted reflection of what I felt for you. And I saw there was only one way out of it—to let her triumph over you. I told her that I loved her. But this was not enough. I must repeat it in front of you. You must witness her triumph. I made it possible. I gave her her great moment. Well, you see what it's done. It freed her so beautifully that she was able to go to Will. They've gone away together. Perfect cure for her as well as for myself.

[*A moment's pause.*]

LEONIE

It all sounds almost too perfect, Kenneth.

KENNETH

I said I didn't expect you to understand it—you have lived always on your emotions. You have never bothered to delve beneath them. You are afraid to, aren't you?

LEONIE

I know this, Kenneth. I heard you say that you loved Paula. I heard your voice. No, I can't accept this, Kenneth! It's not good enough. I've never done that before. I'd only think now that everything you did, everything you said, was to cover what you felt. And I'd end by telling myself that I believed you. I'd end by taking second best from you. No, I must guard myself from that. I felt this a month ago—that's why I sent for Will.

KENNETH

Some day, Leonie, you will learn that feeling is not enough.

LEONIE

But I trust my instinct, Kenneth.

KENNETH

That, Leonie, is your most adorable trait—

LEONIE

What?

KENNETH

That trust—that innocence. If it weren't for that, you wouldn't be you—and everyone wouldn't love you—

LEONIE

Oh, no, Kenneth—
[DENNIS *comes in.*]

DENNIS

Oh, excuse me. But I left my brief-case. Oh, here it is.

[*He picks it up.*]

Without my brief-case I am a man without a Destiny. With it I am—

END OF SUMMER

KENNETH

A man with a brief-case.

LEONIE

[*Crossing rather desperately to* DENNIS—*this straw in the current.*]
What's in it—your stories?

DENNIS

Stories—no, that wouldn't matter. I am fertile; I can spawn stories. But the plans for the magazine are in here—the future of Young America is here—

LEONIE

Will you stay and have a whiskey and soda?

DENNIS

Thanks, but if I do, I shall miss the boat.

LEONIE

Suppose you do?

KENNETH

Leonie—that would delay the millennium one day.

DENNIS

The doctor's right. That would be selfish.

END OF SUMMER

LEONIE

Be selfish. Please stay.

DENNIS

No. Once you are enlisted in a cause, you can't live a personal life. It is a dedication.

LEONIE

Kenneth is leaving. I shall be lonely, Dennis. I can't bear to be alone.

KENNETH

Your need for people is poignant, isn't it, Leonie?

LEONIE

Stay for dinner. After dinner we can talk about your magazine.

DENNIS

Oh, well—that makes it possible for me to stay. Thank you, Kenneth.

[*He goes to sofa, sits, busying himself with briefcase.*]

[*She goes to console to make highball.*]

KENNETH

Send me your magazine, Dennis. I shall be honored to be the first subscriber.

DENNIS

I'll be glad to. Your patients can read it in the waiting-room instead of the *National Geographic*.

KENNETH

Your first subscriber—and very possibly your last.
[*He crosses to door and turns back.*]
Good-bye, Leonie. Good luck, Dennis. We who are about to retire—salute you.
[*She does not look at him. He bows formally to* DENNIS's *back, makes a gesture of "good luck" and exits.*]

DENNIS

Trouble with that fellow is—he lives for himself. No larger interest. That's what dignifies human beings, Leonie—a dedication to something greater than themselves.

LEONIE

[*Coming down to hand him his highball.*]
Yes? Here's your whiskey and soda. I envy you, Dennis. I wish I could dedicate myself to something—something outside myself.

DENNIS

[*Rising to sit beside her.*]
Well, here's your opportunity, Leonie—it's providen-

tial. You couldn't do better than this magazine. It would give you a new interest—impersonal. It would emancipate you, Leonie. It would be a perpetual dedication to Youth—to the hope of the world. The world is middle-aged and tired. But we—

LEONIE

[*Wistfully.*]
Can you refresh us, Dennis?

DENNIS

Refresh you? Leonie, we can rejuvenate you!

LEONIE

[*Grateful there is some one there—another human being she can laugh with.*]
That's an awfully amusing idea. You make me laugh.

DENNIS

[*Eagerly selling the idea.*]
In the youth of any country, there is an immense potentiality—

LEONIE

You're awfully serious about it, aren't you, Dennis?

DENNIS

Where the magazine is concerned, Leonie, I am a fanatic.

END OF SUMMER

LEONIE

I suppose if it's really successful—it'll result in my losing everything I have—

DENNIS

It'll be taken from you anyway. You'll only be anticipating the inevitable.

LEONIE

Why—how clever of me!

DENNIS

Not only clever but graceful.

LEONIE

Will you leave me just a little to live on—?

DENNIS

Don't worry about that—come the Revolution—you'll have a friend in high office.
   [LEONIE *accepts gratefully this earnest of security. They touch glasses in a toast as the curtain falls.*]

CPSIA information can be obtained at www.ICGtesting.com
Printed in the USA
BVOW030323220312

285804BV00005B/61/P

9 781258 181697